Blue Skies
Over Africa

AMBASSADOR

BELFAST, NORTHERN IRELAND
GREENVILLE, USA

Blue Skies Over Africa

ONE WOMAN'S EXPERIENCE OF
GOD'S PROVISION AND PROTECTION

MAIZIE SMYTH
with
VICTOR MAXWELL

AMBASSADOR

BELFAST, NORTHERN IRELAND
GREENVILLE, USA

ISBN 1 84030 132 5

Ambassador Publications
a division of
Ambassador Productions Ltd.
Providence House
Ardenlee Street,
Belfast,
BT6 8QJ
Northern Ireland
www.ambassador-productions.com

Emerald House
427 Wade Hampton Blvd.
Greenville
SC 29609, USA
www.emeraldhouse.com

UFM
47a Fleet Street,
Swindon,
Wiltshire,
SN1 1RE
www.ufm.org.uk

List of Contents

Foreword **7**

Chapter 1   What am I Doing Here? **9**

Chapter 2   In the Shadow of Slemish **15**

Chapter 3   City Life **20**

Chapter 4   Moving On **25**

Chapter 5   The Move **31**

Chapter 6   Language Study **37**

Chapter 7   Setting Foot in Africa **42**

Chapter 8   Bible Study in Bunia **48**

Chapter 9   Government Officials and the Gospel **56**

Chapter 10   Expatriates in Bunia **63**

Chapter 11   Sifu Sifu and Sunday School **69**

Chapter 12   The Highs and Lows of Campus Life **75**

Chapter 13   Kisangani Here We Come **84**

Chapter 14   Are We Still Waiting? **89**

                  Photographic Section **97**

Chapter 15   Am I in God's Place? **113**

Chapter 16   Bible School in Banjwade **121**

Chapter 17   River Region **127**

Chapter 18   Ubundu Visit **139**

Chapter 19   Provision and Protection **145**

Chapter 20   Sleeping Through the Storm **153**

Chapter 21   Bicycles and Bibles in the Bush **160**

Chapter 22   Making Our Lives Count For God **167**

Chapter 23   Strawberry Jam and Tears **173**

Chapter 24   God's Word is Our Rock **181**

Chapter 25   In a Hurry **192**

Chapter 26   War and Want **199**

Chapter 27   Language and Literature **206**

Chapter 28   Every Home in Africa **213**

Chapter 29   Dark Clouds and Blue Skies **223**

Foreword

Reading this book I was not sure whether to laugh, cry or just praise God for all that He has done in the life and ministry of Maizie Smyth.

Brought up as a farmer's daughter in County Antrim, converted in her first year at Secondary School and on leaving school worked in an office in Belfast. It was here that she was first introduced to Mission by attending a UFM prayer meeting.

Shortly after this Maizie felt that God was calling her to full time service and so enrolled at the Bible Training Institute in Glasgow. At school she had not been allowed to take the English language exam because the teacher said that it would be a waste of Government money. In consequence the thought of learning any foreign language was anathema to her. So her first thought was to be a missionary in Southern Ireland with no other language to learn. But God had other plans and He called to Zaire which entailed three languages to master! If you want to read a story that will have you sitting on the edge of your seat, this is it. Laughter, tears, hair raising escapes from danger, God's wonderful protection and blessing and an insight into the church of God in the Congo with its remarkable growth in spite of decades of affliction, then read this book.

A few years ago I was privileged to spend two weeks with Maizie in Kisangani, with a cameraman as we made a film of the work of God in this area. The local security chief gave Maizie permission for us to film and also provided us with a guard, who even turned up for breakfast each day at Maizie's house. One day he said to me that when Maizie dies they will not send her body back to Ireland because she belongs here, we will only send her photograph home!

So read this book and when you have finished reading, pass it on to your church missionary secretary.

Peter Anderson
Christian Ministries
Audio/Visual Director for UFM

1

What Am I Doing Here?

What had I let myself in for? I lay in bed listening to a cacophony of barking dogs almost competing with each other; the repeated crowing of roosters and it was still only 6.00 a.m. I knew I was in Bunia, a rural town of some thirty thousand people in the North Eastern area of Zaire, near to the Ugandan border. *Was this really what God wanted for my life?* The two days since my arrival here as a raw missionary recruit had been filled with meeting people, seeing strange insects and hearing a buzz of strange languages.

Would I ever find my niche here? Would I ever understand all that was going on? I tried to keep these thoughts at bay, but they kept tumbling in upon me like an uninvited avalanche invading my sleep for the first few nights in these strange and new surroundings

From first light the town was a buzz with people going about their business. There was no time to reflect just now. It was time to get up and get going. *A new day...what would this hold?* Just about an hour after sunrise we received news that a senior pastor in Bogoro had died. Bogoro is some twenty-five kilometres from Bunia and I was told that I was expected to travel with my missionary colleagues to the funeral, which would be later that day. (In Zaire, as in most tropical climates, a funeral takes place within twenty-four hours of a person's death). I would not know anyone at the funeral, but protocol demanded that I be there. I was, after all, the latest member of the church to come from *Ulaya* - 'the western world'.

We quickly gathered what we needed for the trip and four of us bundled into my friend Shirley's Volkswagen Beetle and headed out of town. The road, if it could really be called that, was unpaved and resembled a dirt track in an old quarry with rough rocks and gravel strewn here and there. As we jolted from boulder to boulder I could not ignore the magnificent scenery around us. The blue mountain range glistened in the sunshine. Young boys were herding long-horned cattle on the lower slopes. Rounding a few of the many bends, our eyes feasted on the view over the escarpment below which ran right down to Lake Albert. On this clear day even the Ugandan villages on the other side of the lake were visible.

We could not 'dream too long' as we bounced over the bumpy surface. The Beetle made slow progress as it chugged its way up rocky inclines and down the gravel dips for the whole twenty-five kilometres. There was no shade for us from the tropical sun, which was climbing to its noonday zenith. Some young cowboys could be seen taking shelter from the intense sunshine under scantily-leafed bottlebrush trees. Although the little Volkswagen had been a most reliable vehicle in the hot climate it began to cough and splutter as we neared Bogoro and then it unceremoniously died at the side of the road.

What now? Was Shirley a mechanic as well as the many other roles she filled? She seemed so competent as I had watched her tackle so many different tasks during the past two days. *Was this to be another of her gifts?* The answer was no. *Would we wait for a passing motorist to help?* I was told that that was not a practical option for it could take several hours before anyone might pass that way. *What were we to do?*

Shirley and the other missionaries had been along these roads before and they elected that I, being the youngest and most agile lady missionary in the party, should do some research under the vehicle. After an initial protest which was quickly dismissed, I had little option but to agree with them and to have a look under the vehicle. I had recently arrived in Africa and felt I needed to do what I was told by my senior missionary colleagues.

Shirley opened the boot of the car from where she pulled out some sacks which she spread under the car. Unceremoniously lying on my back, I pulled myself into the shade under the vehicle. Looking up at the underside of the vehicle I asked myself, *Why did I not take that car-maintenance course that was advertised back home?*

Initially it was very dark after the glare of the sun, but soon my eyes began to focus as I prayed an urgent prayer to God soliciting divine help for this time of need. To my great amazement I saw that a rubber tube was dripping liquid on to the road. My eyes followed the trickle to the place where the tube had been ruptured. After some discussion, uninvited advice and almost frayed tempers, a temporary repair was made. Shirley had an old piece of bicycle tubing in the car and we were able to do a makeshift job on the spot. On that day I learned that one should never travel in Africa without having several strips of used bicycle tubing.

We were glad to be on our way again, but our happiness was short lived for our repair became unstuck after only five kilometres. At this point we decided to abandon the car and walk the last two kilometres to the church where the funeral service would soon commence.

We knew we were on the correct road for many other people were hurrying on foot in the same direction. Some of these people had emerged out of their small mud huts that lined either side of the rough road. I sort of squirmed when I noticed that most of the pedestrians were barefooted and seemed totally unconcerned that they were walking over the sharp gravel, not to mention their disregard for the hot sun which was beating down on their heads.

As we approached the church the strains of African music was getting louder until it seemed that we were moving in rhythm with the distinctive beat of the drum.

Outside the stone church approximately fifteen or twenty young men were busy preparing a grave in the simple cemetery adjacent to the church. There was no such thing as a mechanical digger. They perspired profusely in the hot sun as they used a hoe and their bare hands to break the hard crust of red clay. Not all the workers could get near the hole in the earth so they rotated in short shifts to dig deeper and prepare for the pastor's interment.

We soon took our places among the hundreds of mourners who had gathered inside the church to sing hymns and glean comfort and assurance from God's Word. Some hymn tunes were familiar and everybody seemed to be singing, but I was struck by the lack of hymnbooks among the crowd. They obviously had memorised the words. Questions began to fill my mind. *Why have they no hymnbooks? Could they not afford them? Are hymnbooks available? Could they read if they had hymnbooks?*

The next thing that struck me was the quality of the pastor's coffin. It was quite an ornate casket such as might be seen in a western city. I am not sure what I had been expecting. Perhaps I thought they would wrap the pastor's remains in banana leaves or in a simple wooden box. *Where did they get such a lovely coffin? Why were two women continually waving a piece of cloth over the open coffin? Why were the women sitting on the floor surrounding the coffin?* Everything was so new to me.

I also noted that no one was dressed in black or in typical mourning attire even though it was a funeral. The ladies were dressed in bright multi-coloured clothes and many of the young men wore bright yellow or red trousers with colourful shirts. Several choirs were crowded near to the front of the church and they were dressed in beautiful bright cotton robes. These choirs sang specially composed songs in tribute to their deceased pastor. Home made harps, guitars and drums accompanied their melodious voices. No one announced anything. One person after another got up to speak, sing or pray, but there was not a moment's silence in it all.

Silence seemed to fall spontaneously when a procession of pastors from the surrounding villages made their way to the seats at the front. While I was drinking in the whole atmosphere I was suddenly startled when a young pastor announced an opening hymn. Another young pastor led the congregational singing as three trumpeters provided added blasts to the musical accompaniment. Some of the hymn tunes were familiar and could easily be recognised as "In the Sweet By and By" or "When the trumpet of the Lord shall sound." This was by no means a mournful service. There was a distinct note of triumph for what God had done through this man's life.

The service was unexpectedly interrupted when four men emerged through the door at the back of the church. Holding a long piece of bamboo stick, they marched straight up through the centre of the congregation towards the open coffin at the front of the church. The women who surrounded the coffin scrambled to their feet to move aside and allow these men to carry out their duties. *What were they doing?* I asked myself. *Could this be some strange tradition?* I discovered they were simply measuring the length and breadth of the coffin so that the grave would be big enough to receive it. I then recognised these young men as part of the grave-digging team I had seen outside.

Although I did not understand what was being said I listened intently and through interpretation I learned that the grave was not yet ready. We would have to remain in the church until they had finished preparing the grave. This meant we had to sing several more hymns, listen to a few more choir pieces and another pastor preached a second sermon. The low backless benches were not the most comfortable to sit on and as time went by I developed pains where I never had pains before. I knew the other missionaries were suffering the same discomfort. For what seemed to be an interminable period, I had to grin and tough it out.

Finally, a signal from outside the church was relayed to the preacher to say that the grave was ready. I imagined that we would now leave the church for the 'burial service'. It was then that the pastor announced that the 'proper service' would begin. We sat there for another three hours while each choir took time to sing their pieces. Added to this, family members and work colleagues needed to pay tribute to their beloved father and respected friend. The preacher certainly was in no hurry when he delivered his lengthy sermon and tribute to the man of God. It was already late afternoon when the funeral cortege finally made its way from the church building to the graveside.

Not being used to such lengthy proceedings at funerals I was a little consoled to know that at least it was only a few yards from the church building to the burial site. Hundreds of people milled around the open grave and with great difficulty the pallbearers forged a way through the crowd to the graveside. When the young men attempted to lower the casket to its last resting-place they discovered they had made a mistake in their measurements. The grave was too short for the coffin. This might have led to further frustration and confusion in any other setting, but this was Africa and the locals were unperturbed. We stood around singing at least five more hymns while the grave-digging team painstakingly lengthened the hole in the ground.

The sun had begun to sink to the horizon and nightfall was nearly upon us when the coffin was finally lowered into the grave. After a brief oration at the graveside the young men lost no time in filling up the grave and piling a mound of red clay where the pastor's remains had been laid to rest. The grieving family continued to be comforted by the many hundreds who gathered to share in their sorrow that day.

This was my first experience of a funeral in Zaire. It sure was a different world. Not all of my questions had been answered, but I concluded that in time I would learn more about daily life in Zaire.

During the time we were in church another missionary colleague, Jay Dee Koscis, had slipped out and went to the rescue of our abandoned Volkswagen. While we sang and perspired in the discomfort and heat of the overcrowded church, he had plenty of time to make a permanent repair job to our vehicle.

Thanks to our missionary colleague our bumpy journey back to Bunia in the dark was trouble free and although we were a little weary we were glad to arrive home in one piece.

After a shower and supper, I lay on my bed that night and reflected on the day. It certainly was eventful. *But*, I concluded, *This is Zaire and I have just witnessed a typical day in the life of a missionary in this part of the world.* I would soon get used to it, but it seemed so far removed from my upbringing in Broughshane, Northern Ireland.

2

In the Shadow of Slemish

County Antrim's Slemish Mountain occupies a very important part in the history of Ireland. On its green and fertile slopes young Saint Patrick, Ireland's Patron Saint, not only tended his sheep during his captivity, but from its elevation he also viewed his native Scotland with longings to return home.

Slemish Mountain and a lower slope known as Collin, also played a big part in my life. Just over six kilometres outside the beautiful village of Broughshane at the foot of Slemish and Collin, my sister Isobel, brother Johnny and I spent long summer days playing or working in the surrounding hay fields of our family home and farm at Greenhill. There we chased sheep and lambs and rounded up cows like regular cowhands and before the days of noisy combine harvesters, we helped bring in the crops.

My early childhood days were still the days of horse-drawn carts and farm implements. There was usually a fight as to which child would be allowed to ride the horse back to his stable. Boredom didn't figure in our vocabulary. Cows had to be hand-milked twice daily, calves fed, chickens tended, not to mention the noisy rumpus of the sows with their litters of piglets. Sheep and lambs presented many a problem as they always wanted to do the opposite of what they were supposed to do. It seemed there was always some work to be done and often we made work-time into playtime as well. Of course, this meant the given task often took a lot longer than my Dad had planned.

On Saturday mornings my father made his weekly trip to the market and before leaving he always left us with our allotted tasks for the morning. Being children, there were some chores we enjoyed more than others. During spring months we had to teach the young calves how to be led on a rope. Brother Johnny and I enjoyed this most of all. We each would take a young calf at the end of a length of rope to a nearby field and put them through their paces. This provided entertainment for us for a couple of hours. After we raced them up and down that field, they knew how to walk or run while having a rope around their neck and head.

One day I became tired of running beside the young calf so decided to mount and ride it just like a horse. Johnny joined in and we had real fun galloping the calves up and down the field. That was until my father appeared at the gate. By then the poor calves were foaming at their mouths while we were hyper with the joy. At the end of the morning I don't know who hurt the most, the young calves from our riding them or Johnny and I from the weight of my father's hand in punishment. We survived and lived to tell the tale - just!

There were also some farm chores I did not like. I specially hated it when I was asked to walk the long distance home from the fields and return with the 'picnic tea' for all the workers. Neither Isobel nor I wanted to do it and we tried every trick we knew to avoid this job.

I was eight years old before Dad bought a tractor to use on the farm. We thought it was a marvel and quite revolutionary. Somehow it did not seem to reduce our workload for we had to rise early every morning to feed the animals and then walk over a mile to school.

Sunday was always different in our house. It was not a day for lying in bed. We had to be up early to milk the cows and feed the animals. We ran around the breakfast table and then got dressed in our Sunday best so that we could make it to church in good time. First Broughshane Presbyterian Church was more than six kilometres away and we had to cycle there and back home again twice on Sundays. This was our weekly social event when fifteen to twenty family members and friends made the return ride from church in Broughshane. Often the banter was sharp or the news and gossip interesting. I don't recall too many theological discussions about the sermon we had just heard at church. On fine summer days it was fun, but on wet days it was more a matter of speed to get home quickly.

Back at the farm no time could be wasted. Lunch was a quick visit to the table and then ready to head out for Sunday School. Thankfully we did not have to make the eight-mile round trip to Broughshane in the afternoon. The church used the facilities at Cross Primary School for the local Sunday School. Most of the children who attended Sunday School were also scholars at this school during the week. I have never forgotten the simple gospel truths we were taught and I cannot remember a time when I did not understand that I was a sinner and needed Jesus Christ to be my Saviour. I seemed to always know that He was the only One who could make me ready to go to heaven.

Even at an early age I wanted to trust the Lord Jesus and invite Him into my heart, but I felt that I was too young to take that step. The longer I hesitated the more I mistakenly reasoned that I should go out and enjoy life first and then, when I was older, I would prepare to meet God.

A great influence on my life at that time was Miss Thompson, the schoolmistress at Cross Primary School. There were only twenty children at our rural school, all of whom were at different stages of their education and represented a cross-section of our community with both Catholic and Protestant children living in blissful harmony. My time at primary school overlapped with my sister Isobel two years ahead of me and my brother Johnny two years behind. Some of our friends were of a different religious persuasion, but it did not seem to be a problem.

Miss Thompson was like a mother to us all. The education authority provided milk daily for children in all schools. At mid-morning break Miss Thompson not only gave us milk, she brought her own large saucepan to school, boiled the milk, and transformed it into drinking chocolate for us all. Hot chocolate was much more tempting than cold milk. On special occasions there may even have been biscuits too. Who could have disliked a school like that?

Besides our usual education of the three "Rs", reading, writing and 'rithmetic, Miss Thompson also faithfully taught us God's Word. Every day I heard of God's love for me. On recollection I think that the school was very appropriately named "*Cross*" Primary School for Miss Thompson began every morning by teaching the Scriptures and never missed an opportunity to teach us about the cross of Jesus Christ.

After seven years at a small rural school, I found the move to the large secondary school in Ballymena to be a traumatic experience. Whatever the weather, I had to cycle to 'The Battery' bus stop where I ditched the bike before catching the bus for the eight-mile journey to Ballymena. Amazingly, all our bicycles were still where we had left them when we returned.

Our home in the evenings was often transformed into a bicycle repair shop as my father coped with the three of us having either brake, steering or puncture problems.

Life at the High School was certainly different too. There was no Miss Thompson and no longer did I know every pupil. Those of us from farms kept close to each other for the 'townies' were quick to make us the brunt of their jokes and ridicule us because we travelled into Ballymena from the countryside. Our accents were also different and we had quite a vocabulary of our own.

During my first year at Secondary School, Faith Mission Pilgrims came to have a tent mission near our home in Greenhill. After most of the farm chores were finished one Sunday evening I decided to go to the small tent. I can't remember who the preacher was, but she spoke from John's Gospel where Jesus said, "I am the door; by me if any man enter in, he shall be saved". I listened intently to the message and knew that God was speaking to me. I was in turmoil. I tried to postpone the matter and argued with myself as to whether or not I should become a Christian that night. Although the battle raged within, I finally decided against taking that step.

The unrest continued in my heart as I made my way home that summer evening. Even though it was late it was still daylight. That meant the hens needed to be rounded up — my allotted task for the evening. I thought I had them all safely into their houses and was about to close up when I discovered one hen still outside and running around the field.

I endeavoured to direct the one stray hen to the little trap door, but in spite of my frantic efforts, she always seemed to go in the opposite direction. I must have chased her round the field for about ten minutes, but all to no avail. It was then it struck me that my pursuit of the hen was a clear picture of my own life. It was so vivid to me. I was the stray and even though God had set before me an open door I persisted in running in the opposite direction. I could not get away from this thought and as soon as the hen was captive and put in the hen house I wasted no time to go to my room. There at my own bedside I knelt down and asked the Lord Jesus to be my Saviour.

In the meeting earlier that evening I had heard that when we invite Jesus into our heart He really comes in, so I simply accepted that. I didn't hear Him come in or feel any different, but I believed He had saved me and had forgiven me. However, I made a mistake that I would live to regret. I resolved not to tell anyone about my conversion. I was afraid that my friends would make fun of me or embarrass me. Furthermore, I didn't see any reason why I should have to tell anyone. I reasoned that religion was a very personal matter that I would keep to myself.

Later, I learned that I was saved and stuck. There was no spiritual growth in my life. Instead of reading God's Word and praying, I lived my life as I pleased. I justified my actions by reasoning that I had 'my ticket' to heaven and that was all that I needed. It was a mistake and I suffered for it.

City Life

Four years at the local Secondary School rolled by very quickly and before I knew it I was faced with the dilemma of choosing a career. I really enjoyed the farm and all the work connected with it, but it was not 'fashionable' for a girl to choose a career in farming. My parents encouraged me to pursue a secretarial course for office work. I enrolled at Ballymena Technical College and during the next two years I acquired skills in shorthand and typewriting. I was soon employed in the office of a dairy firm in Ballymena, but had always wanted to work in Belfast

After one year in Ballymena I started applying for jobs in Belfast and finally ended up in the office of the Down County Education Committee. My sister Isobel had already lived at the Presbyterian Hostel when she went to the city so it was only natural that I also should look for accommodation there. A new job, a new home, in fact everything seemed new as I moved forty-five kilometres from home to spend the weekdays in Belfast.

While staying at the Presbyterian Hostel I met with many Christian young people who were unashamed to openly confess their faith in Jesus Christ. I envied them. Although I taught morning Sunday School at Broughshane Presbyterian Church and at the afternoon Sunday School at Cross when I went home to Greenhill at the weekends, I still was not too keen on telling people I had accepted Jesus Christ as my personal Saviour.

After work it was good to relax during the evenings in the company of these young people who also were away from home and they became my good friends. I soon learned that many of them attended the Christian Endeavour in Berry Street Presbyterian Church where Rev. Glynn Owen was the minister. When they invited me to attend I was happy to go with them. I had only been attending the CE a few weeks when Nancy Bell, one of the leaders approached me and inquired, "You're a Christian, aren't you?"

When I answered positively, she continued, "Will you please open the meeting in prayer." I was terrified. *What had I let myself in for? How was I going to do that?* Until then I had never told anyone that I was a Christian, never mind opening a meeting with prayer. In my panic the only prayer I could think of was Joseph Scriven's great hymn, "What a Friend we Have in Jesus". That prayer was my plunge into the deep end of involvement in the Christian Endeavour group.

The leader's invitation was a spiritual wakeup call and I became aware of my need to grow and develop in my Christian life. I soon learned that this development would not happen without reading and learning more about God's Word, the Bible. Immediately the Scriptures took on a new meaning for me as I accompanied my daily Bible reading with study notes and tried to be sensitive to what God had to say to me.

Prayer also began to take on new meaning in my life. Besides praying for myself I began to pray for my family, for other friends and God's work. At the Christian Endeavour we met various missionaries and Christian workers who solicited prayer for their work. This brought another dimension to intercessory prayer. I then realized that many of the people with whom I worked never went to church and I needed to pray for them and for my witness to them.

Rev. Joe Wright, a former missionary to Brazil and the Irish secretary for Unevangelized Fields Mission, had his office just a few doors from the Presbyterian Hostel in Belfast's Howard Street. He was a very enthusiastic person and although we considered him to be old, a veteran missionary, yet he had a lot of time for young people.

At the hostel Joe introduced us to a monthly prayer meeting for the UFM missionaries all over the world. Some of my newly acquired Christian friends who lived at the hostel attended this meeting and they invited me to go with them. With Joe Wright's missionary experience he realized that the front-line battles are often won through the prayers of home prayer groups. Through that prayer meeting he was giving us opportunity to pray for those who had gone to serve the Lord on the front line.

Due to that prayer meeting, not only did my love for prayer increase, but the geography lessons I had taken at school became more realistic to me. Periodically we had opportunity to meet many missionaries returning home for furlough and listen to them tell of their work in other parts of the world. Perhaps the most thrilling aspect of meeting the missionaries was to hear them tell how God was answering our prayers in Brazil, Zaire or in the Ivory Coast. Their testimonies encouraged us to keep on praying.

I discovered that the more I prayed for the missionaries, the more God was laying another burden on my heart. God challenged me to do something to help them. *Could I help financially?* I knew I could give some of my wages to help those who had gone with the gospel. There were many needs and I began to help out with some of them. I soon realized that there was great joy in giving to God's Work. This was all part of a learning process of walking with God and I was enjoying getting to know Him better.

There was also an opportunity to meet missionaries at the Berry Street Christian Endeavour meetings. Dorothy Moffat, our CE Missionary Convenor, invited a different missionary speaker each month. Some were from abroad while others worked in Northern Ireland. A visit from Fred Rainey of CEF in October 1966 made an indelible impression upon me. The nation was in mourning after the terrible disaster at Aberfan in the Welsh valleys when a slagheap gave way and engulfed a primary school in the town. Over one hundred and forty children lost their lives.

Fred had come to speak to us about the children of Belfast and understandably there was a sombre mood in the meeting because of the disaster. He closed with this challenge "If Aberfan had happened on your street, how many boys and girls would be in heaven today because you had led them to Christ?"

By this time I had left the Presbyterian hostel and had moved into an apartment with two friends in a residential area of Belfast. Many boys and girls played on our streets, but I had never told them of Jesus. Even though I was teaching in Sunday School at home in Broughshane, I had not been involved in trying to reach children in Belfast.

At the end of that meeting I was so challenged about what had been said I decided to speak to Fred. I asked if there was any possibility of helping to teach God's Word to the boys and girls in South Belfast where I lived. He not only assured me there were plenty of opportunities, but within a few weeks he made it possible for me to start teaching in the children's meetings at McClure Street City Mission Hall.

Fred and Violet Rainey also introduced me to Child Evangelism Fellowship teacher training classes, which specialise in equipping would-be helpers for children's work. These classes marked another milestone in my spiritual development. I found that when I studied God's Word in preparation to teach the children, God was also teaching His Word to me. The classes also helped me prepare better lessons for the children at the Broughshane and Cross Sunday Schools where I continued to teach every week.

The challenge of teaching others increased even more at the beginning of Ulster's 'troubles' in 1969. McClure Street had been a Protestant district, but over the previous few years many Catholic families had moved in and it was now considered to be a 'mixed' community area. We were able to pack over one hundred children from both communities into the hall every Thursday night, the majority being from Catholic families. Besides singing gospel choruses and learning the memory verses, these children were instructed in the Scriptures and left in no doubt that Jesus Christ was the only way to the Father and to heaven. It gave me great satisfaction and joy to be serving the Lord in this way.

Not all the children professed faith in Jesus Christ and we were sorry to see many of them persist in their own way instead of putting Jesus Christ first in their lives. A sense of eternity was impressed upon all the children and us as workers when a motor accident on McClure Street left a little six-year-old boy dead. When we visited the home to express our sincere sympathy the parents told us how their little boy came home from the Thursday meetings and taught his mother the choruses or memory verse he had learned. She particularly liked to hear him singing the little chorus 'One way God said to get to heaven; Jesus is the only way'.

The McClure Street City Mission Hall does not exist any longer, but I know that eternity will reveal the impact of that Thursday night children's meeting. Not only were the Ormeau Road children and the boys and girls at Broughshane learning God's Word, but unwittingly I also was growing in the Lord. I was not aware that He was preparing me for other avenues of service.

4

Moving On

Having been raised on a farm I calculated that I was not afraid of a bit of hard work. However, chasing animals in the hills and fields near Broughshane could never have prepared me for chasing after fifty boys and girls at a week's camp in Tollymore Forest Park near Newcastle, Co Down. Besides trying to sleep under canvas we also had to make sure that the campers slept when they were supposed to be sleeping. Attending to the upkeep of the improvised sanitary conveniences for such a crowd of children was another difficult and unwelcome chore.

All would have been fine if the weather had been kind to us, but with several days of rain, life was frustrating to say the least. This frustration was compounded when the children decided to play in the muddy field while the rain pelted down on them. They thought it was the best fun they had all week, but some fine weather made for excellent sports activities with crafts and other projects which we carried out in the main tent.

Meal times were enjoyable as we spread the table three times a day for fifty hungry little mouths with ravenous appetites. The afternoon games and competitions were sandwiched in between the morning Bible studies and evening devotions. Many parents often joined us for the evening sessions.

Leaders and campers alike enjoyed these 'holidays' and many friendships were formed. Undoubtedly the highlight of camp was when boys and girls recognised their need of Jesus Christ and trusted Him as Saviour. Many of these children attended our Good News clubs, so we had opportunity to follow them up in the weekly meetings.

Since arriving in Belfast I had been driving a little blue four-seater Ford Anglia car. After several years on the road in and around Belfast transporting people to and from meetings at McClure Street or Berry Street, and the weekly eighty-kilometre round trip to Broughshane and back, my little car was beginning to show signs of 'old age.' However, by this time I was well established in the offices of the Down County Education Committee where I earned a reasonable salary. I thought it was time I should be thinking of buying a new car.

This was the age of the famous Mini car and a brand new one really appealed to me. To justify the purchase I reasoned in my mind that the Lord would undoubtedly want me to have this car since I transported so many people to and from various meetings. After all, I was using it for His Work and I was sure He would approve of my driving a decent car. I further reasoned that the camp holidays were a good time to start saving as they were not financially draining. I started my personal project to purchase a car.

At this time God challenged me about those with whom I worked every day. Between Sunday Schools and children's meetings, plus trying to continue my link at Berry Street Presbyterian Church, most of my free time was totally committed to Christian service. However, God showed me that those with whom I worked also needed the Lord. It weighed on my heart when I prayed and I kept asking the question, "How can I share the gospel with them?" I sought to live out my Christian life in the office and many recognised this. Often when a member of staff used a curse word they would look at me and apologise. Frequently we had 'theological' discussions during our tea break and they knew what I thought of God and the gospel, but I wanted them to understand the gospel for themselves.

My musings and prayers seemed to be answered when it was announced that an evangelistic mission was to be conducted at the nearby Great Northern Street City Mission Hall. My work colleagues became prayer targets and when the meetings commenced I invited them to attend. I was a little apprehensive about this, but was thrilled when several of them accepted the invitation and agreed to go with me.

As the date arrived I intensified my prayer efforts for those who had planned to attend the meetings and hoped they would hear a good presentation of the gospel. That evening the preacher's text was from Luke 12:15 "Take heed, and beware of covetousness: for a man's life consisteth not in the abundance of the things which he possesseth." The preacher went on to explain how material goods can take the first place in our lives and therefore rob God of His rightful place. As I listened to the message I was a little disappointed that it was not a direct a gospel message which I would have liked them to hear. None of my friends seemed to be in anyway moved by the preacher or his preaching and soon they made their way home.

That night I reflected on the preacher's sermon and specially the text, "Take heed, and beware of covetousness: for a man's life consisteth not in the abundance of the things which he possesseth." I felt an opportunity had been missed to reach those girls for the Saviour and was asking why God had not spoken to them. It then hit me that maybe the word was for me instead of them? *For me? But Lord, I am a Christian.* It was then I felt as though the Lord was putting His finger on my plans to buy that new mini. I tried to dismiss the thought as being ridiculous and reflected on the justifiable reasons I had previously considered.

Next Sunday morning I was dumbfounded when I went to First Broughshane Presbyterian Church and the Rev. Porter preached from Luke 12:15, the same text. *Was this really God speaking to me? Was He testing me?* I reasoned that I was obeying the Lord in all I was doing and He could not be specifically speaking to me.

I suffered another hammer blow that same Sunday when I attended Berry Street Presbyterian. At the service the minister announced that he was going to speak on "Take heed, and beware of covetousness: for a man's life consisteth not in the abundance of the things which he possesseth." I had heard three sermons on the same text in as many days. By that time I felt that God was not so much speaking to me, He was shouting at me.

I was humiliated and a battle raged in my heart during that third meeting. I returned to the apartment alone and was content that the other girls had still not returned from their weekend at home. I went to my bedroom and there poured out my heart before God. Being Ballymena-born and bred, I was used to bargaining. As a child I heard my parents on many occasions bargaining for good prices for my new shoes or clothes. In my teenage years I was to discover that this was not so in other areas. When on a shopping trip with my elder sister to Belfast, I purchased a pair of shoes. On paying I duly asked the usual Ballymena question, "How much reduction will you give me?" My blushing sister quickly changed the subject of conversation with the chain store assistant. Once outside I heard clearly that one does not bargain with set prices in the big city.

In a similar way, I tried to bargain with God that night. I wanted to serve Him, but I wanted to hold on to what was mine, my ways, my plans, and my money. I was in great turmoil and as the conflict came to a head I surrendered everything to Him as best I knew how, even my plans for the new mini. It seemed I spent a long time in the Lord's presence sorting out my financial affairs.

As a result of that encounter with God and the full and final surrender to Him, I shared most of my savings with the various missionaries with whom I had become involved. Some of those savings for the mini even went to Zaire to help UFM missionaries there. I reasoned that I could start afresh to save up for my new mini. I did feel however, that the Lord permitted me to retain enough money for a conference holiday in England, which I had already booked and it was only two weeks away.

The conference was a refreshing time of Bible teaching and fellowship. One day, at the conference I was sitting at lunch when a complete stranger started chatting to me. He was a missionary with

CEF which meant we had a lot in common. Our conversation covered general topics about God's work and the Bible studies we were enjoying. In the middle of his conversation he said to me, "If you ever think of going to Bible School you might consider the Bible Training Institute in Glasgow."

I listened to what he said, but thought he was obviously an ex-student from there doing his publicity stunt. I quickly replied that I had no intention of going to Bible School. After I left the dining table I chuckled to myself *Maizie Smyth go to Bible School? The Lord would never ask me to do a thing like that. Bible School is for others, not for me.*

As the conference progressed various speakers referred to the same theme the stranger had touched on at the meal table. In my heart I began to think, *Maybe the thought wasn't so ridiculous after all!* By Saturday night when I was returning to Belfast alone on the Liverpool boat, the thought of going to Bible School had become a major issue in my thinking. *Could God be asking me to go to Bible School? No. Not me. Definitely not me.*

There was little sleep on the ten-hour overnight voyage. I was not satisfied with my dismissive reply to the question. There was still a nagging doubt in the back of my mind; *could God really be asking me to leave my work and go to Bible School? What would that mean? Would I become a missionary?*

Since Joe Wright got us praying for missionaries I had taken great interest in missionary activity. I really admired how my various missionary friends seemed so fulfilled in their work. However, I also was fulfilled and quite happy to work for God on a 'part-time' basis in the children's clubs, Sunday Schools and various missionary prayer groups. But the controversy persisted; *was God now asking more from me? Impossible!* It was then I remembered how I had surrendered all to Him in my bedroom just a few weeks earlier. Submissively I bowed before the Lord and yielded again to whatever the will of God might be.

Alone in my little cabin that night I made a pact with God. I told Him I needed to be clear on what He was saying to me. If it was to be Bible School then I needed to be absolutely certain. I asked the Lord to do one of two things to confirm to me that this indeed was

His way. I was very happy in my job. I didn't think I had done anything wrong before going on holiday, but if God really wanted me in Bible School then He would have to put me out of my job. Failing that He could put me out of the house which I was sharing with my two friends. Even as I made this pact with God I thought either of these propositions was impossible. My job was secure for life and the accommodation was home from home. My friends and I shared the upper two floors of a house whilst the owner made her home on the ground floor. We treated her well, doing various chores for her and sat with her in the evenings. She knew she could never find better tenants than us. Therefore, I was sure there was no way she would want to put us out of our home.

The pact with God completed, I slept for the rest of the journey to Belfast. Soon I was back home at the apartment where I shared with my two friends all the excitement of the holiday. I never mentioned my 'pact with God'. In fact, I said nothing about Bible School or how God had been speaking. That was a matter between God and myself.

As we sipped an early morning cup of tea one of them spoke and said, "Maizie, things have changed a little here since you left. The elderly owner of this house believes it is time for her to sell it and move nearer to her son in England. The continuing troubles in Ireland are making her more afraid to remain in Belfast. She has given us one month to look for another house."

I was speechless. My head went into a whirl. Although I was stunned that we would be losing our comfortable home, I was even more amazed that God had answered me so clearly and so speedily. I was in no doubt as to what He was asking of me. God was really speaking to me and in a very clear manner.

Now I knew I needed to move, but where to?

5

The Move

Still reeling from the shock that God should actually be speaking to me about going to Bible School, I tried to come to terms with the implications of it all. Day after day I continued to devour God's Word. The more I read the more I was convinced this was His call on my life. I knew I needed to take some practical steps to follow this leading, but was not too sure what I should do. The thought of Bible School and study made me shudder. I thought of a hundred reasons why I was not a suitable candidate for such an institution. After all, I had only secretarial training and I thought that would be of little use to anyone on the mission field. Furthermore, Bible School fees were high and I had no money for I had emptied my bank balance at God's prompting just a few weeks previously. It struck me that maybe I should be thinking of working for one year and then going to Bible School. My mind mulled over all these reasons and many more, but in my heart of hearts I knew God was asking me to take a step of faith and trust Him.

When I finally gave in to trusting God to lead me step by step, I wrote to three different Bible Schools requesting details of their courses, one of which was the Bible Training Institute in Glasgow.

After receiving the relevant literature I prayed and tried to decide which Bible School I should go to, but only became more confused. One Sunday evening I wanted to put the whole matter out of my mind so I picked up a book recounting the testimony of Ulster's famous evangelist of an earlier generation, W. P. Nicholson. I had heard many stories of how outspoken and uncouth he could be and for some reason I thought he had never gone to Bible School. The book corrected my mistaken perceptions and I was shocked to read that W. P. had trained at Glasgow's B.T.I. It seemed that consistently this particular college was brought to my attention. Before retiring later that night I read Psalm 32. I was drawn to verse eight, "I will instruct thee and teach thee in the way which thou shalt go; I will guide thee with mine eye." This was another confirmation to me that God was definitely leading me to B.T.I..

During the following week I was invited to go to Glasgow for an interview. As I had already taken all my annual leave from work and was planning to leave my employment it was impossible for me to attend the interview. When I explained my predicament, the staff at B.T.I. informed me that they would be in touch with me. A few days later a letter arrived with the following news:

> "You are accepted to commence at B.T.I. at the beginning of September. We will interview you on your arrival here. We note, however, that you have no money for fees, but you say that you have faith. If you have faith for September you can have it for August and we are therefore asking you to forward one term's fees (£125) before the end of August."

That letter was received on a Monday morning at the end of July. I panicked a little. *What was I to do now?* I didn't have money for one week's fees let alone one term! This was my first big hurdle. I felt I had given all my money to God and His work and here I was left high and dry without the required fees.

Thoughts and prayers mingled in my mind during my quiet times and throughout the day. I tossed and turned at night with the same thoughts; *Hadn't God called? Really God, it is your problem and I am going to leave it with You.*

On the next day I gave notice to the Down County Education Committee that I would be leaving my employment at the end of August. No one in the office had any idea that I was even thinking of going to Bible School. When my letter arrived on the Director's desk I was summoned to his office. "You cannot possibly leave now," was his remark. "We are about to re-organise the system and seeing you have been here for many years and know how it works we really need you to stay. Couldn't you please delay your departure for one year?"

It is amazing the number of escape routes that appear when we want to do God's bidding. I listened to the Director, but insisted I was leaving at the end of August as stated in the letter. By lunchtime the news was out. "This piece of office furniture is going to Bible School." was the whisper that went round the staff.

The dining hall was in a buzz with this news. Many surprised colleagues came to inquire if the 'grapevine' was giving the correct news. "Yes, I am going to Bible School." I confidently replied without knowing where and how it was all going to happen.

One Christian colleague from another department asked me to stop by his office to chat with him. After lunch I dropped in to see him and was surprised when he emotionally told me how God had called his son to go to Bible School many years ago and as a father he had put barriers in his way. He counselled his son to seek a career first. He was broken as he continued to tell me that the lad was now far from God. The distressed man blamed himself for his son's waywardness. He proceeded to say that he felt God was giving him a second chance to help someone else go to Bible School. With that he reached me an envelope and said, "That will help you some way along the line. May God bless you."

I was a little embarrassed, but felt sorry for this broken-hearted father. After I withdrew from his office I returned to my desk and opened the envelope. Out fell a cheque for £125. I wept with joy. Not only did I know that God had called me, but now within a few hours of handing in my notice to terminate employment, my first term's fees were already provided. I remembered what I had read in Jeremiah 29:11; "For I know the plans I have for you, declares the

Lord, plans to prosper you and not to harm you, plans to give you hope and a future."

It was difficult to settle back into my duties at the office that afternoon. I was so excited and my mind was racing as I recalled how good God was. Again I had discovered that when I trust Him, His way is definitely far better than I could ever imagine.

However, there were still many hurdles to overcome before going to Glasgow. Earlier I had worried about telling my family and friends that I was leaving to go to college, but when the time came I discovered that God had prepared them for what was to come. During the previous few years I had close associations with CEF and UFM, but I was determined not to be pulled or biased in either direction as I was anxious to respond to God's call to whatever or wherever that should be. I was confident that the Lord would lead me in His way and that was all I wanted.

September arrived too quickly and before I knew it I was sitting in a class with thirty-five other first-year students in B.T.I.. The five-story sandstone building located in Bothwell Street, downtown Glasgow, was adjoined to the Christian Institute and YMCA and was affectionately known among the students as "The Old Grim Castle". After ten years away from a school desk it was not easy adapting to studying again. English had not been my best subject at school and now with an unending list of essays and reading assignments I definitely needed the Lord's help. Added to these pressures were participation in evangelistic outreach in several rundown areas of Glasgow and adapting to communal living. There were lots of other new experiences which brought a mixture of joy and trials.

One of the early lessons I learned was that not all Christians hold to the same customs and priorities as we do in Northern Ireland. While the majority of students were from the British Isles I met other fine Christians from many foreign countries. All of these students were preparing for Christian ministry, but they did not always see things the way I saw them. However, I could not deny their love for the Saviour and learned to appreciate the grace of God in their lives. At the same time I had great difficulty sorting out in my mind what was biblical, what was cultural and what was traditional. These early lessons at the B.T.I. were not wasted in years to come.

I was assigned to a practical outreach team to work in Glasgow's notorious Gorbals area, which was the most rundown district of the city. Everyone warned me how difficult Christian work would be in the Gorbals. We had to wait a couple of weeks for a new pastor to be installed in the Glasgow Medical Mission which would serve as the base for our outreach. When he did arrive he shared his testimony and I could not believe what I was hearing. The new Pastor's name was Bill Gilvear and he had just arrived home from Zaire where he had been a missionary with UFM. I thought it was more than coincidental that I had been assigned to work with someone from UFM. Had I not gone to great pains before leaving home to cut off my links with UFM? Without solicitation the Mission was back on my doorstep.

That outreach ministry was a real training ground for me. We visited the newly constructed high-rise apartment blocks, made contacts with non-church goers and helped in children's clubs and youth groups. It was great to see some people trust the Saviour. We found many lonely and distressed people during the outreach. Bill gave us pastoral care and was very helpful and most encouraging. In our team we had great times of fellowship and prayer and Bill was always interested in God's leading in our lives.

Between the school's academic terms I spent the summers working with CEF in Southern Ireland. These camps and clubs also provided me with very practical training, but soon it was back to books and lectures at the Old Grim Castle for another year. I studied theology, surveyed the Bible, learned about church history and memorised words I had never heard of before. It was all part of the college course.

All too soon three years at B.T.I. were coming to an end. Exams completed and a diploma to say that I had finished the course well. However, again I was at a crossroad and faced the question, *What next*? I knew where I wanted to go and why? I had my heart set on the South of Ireland for I knew I would not have to learn a foreign language. Every mission field outside Ireland seemed to require at least one other language and Maizie Smyth knew her limits. English was hard enough for a farm girl from Broughshane. The sensible option was to aim for Southern Ireland. I convinced myself that this surely would be God's choice too.

But would it be?

6

Language Study

One Monday evening during those final days in Glasgow, we returned to the Mission from our visitation in the Gorbals. Bill Gilvear asked me if I was going to the UFM Missionary Weekend at Netherhall in Largs, the following weekend. I told him I had not made any plans to go, but I knew it would provide a lovely weekend away from the Old Castle. Bill pressed further inquiring if my reason for not going was due to lack of money. I did not give a direct answer, but his guess was not far from the truth.

Little more was said, but in his prayer at the end of the evening Bill asked the Lord to send me the money for the missionary conference by the next morning. I was not too comfortable about Bill's prayer for I did not particularly want to go to the conference. I knew that at the conference there would be great emphasis on serving God on one of the UFM fields and by this time I had firmly set my mind on going to the South of Ireland with CEF. *How dare Bill or anyone try and upset my plans*?

Next morning I received a note from a lady in Belfast in which she wrote, "The Lord has shown me that you will need this." Inside the envelope was a gift, which was the exact amount I needed for the conference weekend. Bill's prayer had been answered without any manipulation from him or agreement from me. Now my thinking changed, *How could I not go to the conference?* During that missionary weekend I heard about Zaire over and over again. It was very challenging and inspiring. Several bloody revolutions had left the country in a sad state of political unrest. The national Christians and missionaries had survived terrible days of brutal persecution during which many foreigners and nationals had been killed. Now, just ten years after the rebellion, missionaries were urgently needed to meet the demands of the growing church. I listened to the challenge, but answered in my heart, *No Lord, I couldn't go there.* The speakers spoke of using Swahili, French and Lingala as the languages of communication. I had already declared there was definitely no way I could learn one foreign language. These missionaries had to learn three alien tongues. I concluded this was not for Maizie Smyth.

As if the Lord was answering my protest Psalm 32:8 kept repeating in my head; "I will instruct thee and teach thee in the way which thou shalt go; I will guide thee with mine eye." For over a week there was a daily struggle about Zaire, the need for missionaries there and what the Lord wanted me to do about it. I told the Lord that I was only a secretary and what He needed in Zaire were linguists, doctors, nurses or teachers. There was no way He would want me there.

At B.T.I. on Friday mornings we had the missions lecture and frequently a missionary came to that class and spoke of their work. On the Friday following the conference I was still agitated about what I had heard at the meetings and what I should do. I was shocked when I discovered that the speaker at the missions lecture was a missionary from Zaire although he worked with another mission. To be truthful, I found his talk quite boring, but his finishing statement hit home; "You may not be a doctor, nurse or teacher, but you can communicate the gospel. In Zaire today God needs people who know they are called by Him and those who can reach out to all levels of the community." I was dumbfounded.

Other students went to the next lecture, but I made a hasty retreat to my room where I wept uncontrollably. Now I knew God was calling me to Zaire. God's call was becoming louder and increasingly clear each time. My focus changed from *Did God want me to go?* to, *Was I willing to go?* There definitely was no way I could go in my own strength. Through my tears I surrendered again to His will. I confessed that I was nothing, but was willing to be used by Him. Still on my knees before God I read Joshua 1:9; "Be strong and of a good courage; be not afraid, neither be thou dismayed: for the Lord thy God is with thee whithersoever thou goest". What more could I ask from God? Like Joshua, to whom the original promise had been given, I just had to step out by faith on the promise and trust in God.

My friends were as amazed as I was that I should be going to Zaire. During the final days of June 1976 I was occupied with completing application papers to the Unevangelized Fields Mission and doing final exams at B.T.I.. From Glasgow I went to the CEF Summer Institute for two months. Because of my association with CEF many friends concluded I would go to work among the boys and girls in Southern Ireland. Until a few months earlier I also was sure of this move, but the Lord had changed all that.

However, I found my call being tested over and over again. Perhaps I let my own thoughts haunt me at times. Well-meaning people confronted me dozens of times with the inevitable question, "Why are you not going to Southern Ireland with CEF?" The answer was very simple, "Because God has called me to Zaire." However, the repeated questions put my call to the test and confirmed to me that God was leading me to Zaire.

Following the application to the UFM I was invited to London for initial interviews which were very positive. The next hurdle was to accompany several other applicants on the two-week Candidates Course at the UFM HQ in London. This course was designed by the UFM as 'getting to know the mission' and the mission 'getting to know the candidate'. Jill Thompstone had recently returned from Zaire and was one of the hostesses at the course. She also gave lectures on various aspects of missionary life in Africa. Her slide presentation gave a clear picture of life in Zaire.

All the other candidates were destined for Brazil so I had a particular interest in Jill and was able to spend quite a lot of time with her. The more I saw of her work the more I realised that she was so talented in many different ways. I made the mistake of comparing myself with her and soon came to the conclusion that God had made one big mistake. I could never do what Jill did. Now I was more than ever sure that I never could be a missionary in Zaire.

The Candidates Course ended with individual interviews with the Mission's Candidates Council for each prospective missionary. On the night prior to those interviews I was again wrestling in prayer before God. I was convinced I was not a suitable candidate for Zaire. I had already proved that God's Word was always there to guide me so that night, on my knees, I read these words, "You are my servant; I have chosen you and have not rejected you. So do not fear, for I am with you; do not be dismayed, for I am your God. I will strengthen you and help you; I will uphold you with my righteous right hand." (Isaiah 41:9-10). This was God's unmistakable answer to my doubts and misgivings. It was an appropriate and personal word to me and armed with these promises I was prepared for the final interviews the next morning. By the time they were over I was pronounced an accepted missionary candidate with the UFM for Zaire.

French is the official language of Zaire and the Mission sent me to undertake an eight-month course at a Language School in the French Alps. During those days I grappled with phonetics, the past, present and future tenses of regular and irregular verbs and other aspects of French grammar. Learning the rudiments of grammar and written French was much preferred to the nightmare of learning phonetics and spoken French. One Monday it had been a particularly gruelling morning as the teacher tried to help me with pronunciation. The poor teacher needed a lot of patience and courage to teach a Broughshane woman to pronounce simple phonetic sounds. After each session with the teacher I was convinced I would never get this language properly.

Coffee time was a welcome break from the classes and an opportunity to read whatever mail might have arrived. That particular Monday morning amongst other letters there was one for me from the UFM. The first paragraph of that letter left me stunned and discouraged:

"We at UFM regret to tell you of our decision to withdraw from working with the church in the Zaire field. This will mean that you will not be able to go to Zaire as originally planned."

I don't recall if I read any more of that letter. I hurried to my room and again tears flowed freely. I was devastated. Language study was discouraging, but now I was sure I had made a big mistake. I kept asking the Lord why He had let me come this far?

After the initial shock, the only place I knew to turn to was God's Word. *Would God have something to say to me?* Much time that day was spent in prayer, reading the Bible and trying to reason things out. The only consoling word that came to me during those hours was from Revelation 3:7-8; "These are the words of him who is holy and true, who holds the key of David. What he opens no one can shut, and what he shuts no one can open….See, I have placed before you an open door that no one can shut. I know that you have little strength."

My heart was at peace with Him and I had the assurance He would lead me in His Way wherever that was. My responsibility was to obey His Word and walk closely with Him. I had many questions in my mind, but I knew He would work it all out. Perhaps the burning question that confronted me most was, *How was God going to open the door to Zaire?*

7

Setting Foot in Africa

At the language school I continued to grapple with grammar and phonetics whilst dealing with shocking news that the door to Zaire had apparently closed. Despite my difficulties, I received my diploma for French with a 'distinction' grade. Only the Lord could have brought me through those eight months and by the conclusion of the course I was enjoying speaking French. I was far from being a 'good French speaker', but at least I could understand most conversations and make myself understood.

While I was studying grammar the Mission had been in negotiations with the Zairian Church in relation to the future role and ministry of their missionaries. The Theological School at Bunia and Mission Hospital at Nyankunde, jointly managed by the leadership from several evangelical ministries, were still open for us, but we were required to be seconded to this work by another missionary society other than our own.

Under this arrangement I was nominated to be part of a team that would work in Bunia and Nyankunde under the umbrella of the Africa Inland Mission (AIM). This truly was an answer to prayer not only for myself, but also for several UFM missionaries who had already worked in Zaire.

It was with mixed emotions that I said good-bye to family and friends in October 1978, and with the barrels packed I left Broughshane for service in Zaire. It was not easy leaving home and yet there was excitement in looking forward to finally getting to the place where God had called me to work.

As I took the overnight flight from London to Nairobi many questions were flooding my mind. *Could I cope with the heat? Where would I live? Would I live alone or share a house with someone? What about all those insects they told me about?* In London I had been warned to beware of all sorts of beasties from mosquitoes to snakes. I think they were trying to frighten me. I had been told I would be working at the Theological Seminary, but I had not received a job description. A board representing several evangelical missions, UFM, WEC, Conservative Baptists, Brethren and AIM, jointly managed the Theological Seminary.

During the nine-hour flight sleep eluded me, either because of fear or excitement or perhaps a mixture of both. I was still awake when the captain announced that we were approaching Nairobi Airport.

The AIM have a good 'service system' in operation to receive missionaries coming to Africa and I was so pleased to see Jim Kingma at Nairobi airport holding a board with my name on it. He had made reservations for me to stay for one night at the AIM guesthouse in Nairobi before being whisked off the next morning on the MAF plane to Bunia.

I had no idea what to expect on arrival in Zaire. It was great to meet Shirley Chumley at the Bunia airport. Shirley would be my housemate for the next two years. It was evident she knew her way around the airport protocol and competently handled the officialdom. I felt totally lost.

For eight months I had studied French and thought I was well equipped to communicate with the Zairians, but after a short while in the country I realised that very few of them were speaking French. I soon learned that on meeting someone, the first phrase is usually communicated in French but then conversation switches to Swahili. That meant I had to learn another language!

That first evening the missionaries living in Bunia gave a little reception party to welcome this new missionary into their group. It was great to meet them all and to be able to set up a meeting with the field leader, Don Dix. He was the man who would outline my job description.

The next few days were spent meeting people, mainly church leaders, as Bunia was the headquarters of the African Inland Churches. I felt welcome amongst them and it was obvious they were a happy people despite their lack of material goods. I was impressed by how much laughter was interjected into their conversations.

During those first days there were many new things to learn; sleeping under mosquito nets; boiling and filtering all drinking water; ironing all clothes thoroughly to kill off the mango flies which laid their eggs on the washing as it hung on the line to dry; buying goods in bulk. There were no petrol stations so we bought fuel in forty-gallon drums and then had to filter it before it could be used. The heat was not too severe as I had arrived in the wet season. However, during tropical downpours I needed Wellington boots more often than sandals to walk the roads, which became a virtual quagmire with streams of water coursing everywhere.

Arrangements were made for me to study Swahili at Rethy, an AIM station some one hundred and twenty kilometres north of Bunia. My teacher was to be Miss Burnetta Wambold who had taught in the primary schools in Zaire for over forty years. If anyone knew how to teach, it must surely be her.

When I arrived at the school two MAF workers were struggling with Swahili. Miss Burnetta used the old method of learning lists and lists of vocabulary and these MAF personnel did not agree with this method. They had been there two weeks and before starting had told Burnetta that they didn't want to spend too much time on the study programme. They said "What we want is a crash course." Doesn't sound too appropriate for MAF workers, but this was language study and not flying lessons!

On the morning I arrived they had told Burnetta that they would not continue with their lessons. Burnetta simply looked at them across her large mahogany desk and commented "You did tell me that you wanted a crash course, but I didn't think you would crash so soon!"

I arrived that afternoon and a disgusted Burnetta met me at the airstrip. We were introduced to each other as the pilot got my bag out of the hold of the five-seater MAF plane. After we were introduced Burnetta said to me, "Make up your mind right now if you are going to study or not. If you're not willing to study then just go back home on the plane you came on and don't waste my time."

I wondered how I was going to survive the next three months; the time assigned to learn Swahili. I not only survived those three months, but thoroughly enjoyed them and also learned Swahili.

Burnetta and I became firm friends, although she did push me to my limits. Each day began with one hour of study and then three hours of homework before lunch. The process was repeated in the afternoon and so by nightfall my head was buzzing. I had been studying for eight days when a primary school principal arrived during one of my lessons. He talked with Burnetta in French so that I could follow the conversation. He asked Burnetta if I could come and do a Bible lesson at his school once a week. As I listened it became evident that the teaching was to be in Swahili. I protested in every way I could, but Burnetta quickly reminded me that I was the student and would do as the teacher said. The end of story was that I had to start the next week. When I inquired how this would be possible considering she had just put a red pen through all of the last night's homework, she replied , "All the grammar was correct, but it stinks of the white man."

She instructed me that I was to prepare the Bible lessons at the school, she would correct them and then I would have to memorise them in order to give the message to the children. That sounded a lot of work with a lot of loopholes, but Burnetta insisted, "I am the teacher and you are the student."

There was no way I could protest further. As it was near to Christmas I decided to give lessons on the birth of Christ. During the third week I was in full flow, in the middle of my lesson, with a hundred and fifty children listening intently, when a few of them began to snigger. I looked to the principal and in French asked, "Did I make a mistake?"

He simply replied, "No. Continue."

I knew I had made some mistake, but at my next phrase the class went into hysterics. Once again I asked him to interpret what I had said but he insisted I was to continue with the lesson.

It was impossible to continue. I discovered that when I told of the angel announcing Christ's birth the host of angels singing, that the actual interpretation of the word I had used for angel was runner bean! In effect, what I had said was that a runner bean announced that Christ was born and then the heavens were full of runner beans!

The children soon settled down again and the lesson continued. I don't know the result of my lessons on those young children's hearts, but they surely gave me a great base for learning Swahili. Burnetta was a tough taskmaster, but an excellent teacher. Instead of the three months that I was allotted for studying Swahili, I was taking my final exams after seven weeks. I knew the grammar and had a limited vocabulary, but also knew that with time I would build up that vocabulary.

When I returned to Bunia I planned to spend one week going over all my notes to make sure I understood all the grammar. I arrived back in Bunia late on Thursday evening. It was great to be back to the room where I had spent my first few days in Bunia. Bunia would be my home for the next ten years. The house was on the Seminary Campus and this meant that there was constant contact with the students and their families.

I had planned my programme of study, but before I even started it early on the Friday morning, Dr. Marini Bodho, who was then Director of the Seminary, came to tell me of a crisis they had in the women's Bible School. Someone was unable to teach the Pauline Epistles and he was wondering if I could fill in for them. As he talked it became evident that the classes were in Swahili and he was expecting me to start on Monday. I realised this was the work the Lord had brought me to do in Zaire, but I wondered how I would tell him that I wasn't ready for it yet.

Unable to refuse his request, I agreed with much trepidation to give the lessons. This proved to be very beneficial for my cultural adaptation in the country and further language study. I am not sure who gained the most benefit from those Bible School classes. For the majority of ladies in the class, Swahili was probably their third language. They understood the Swahili of the street, the market and the home, but when we got into God's Word that was a different vocabulary. There were so many words they did not understand and with my limited vocabulary I had difficulty trying to explain them.

I was asked to begin teaching Ephesians and soon ran into difficulty in Chapter 1:14 where it speaks of the Holy Spirit, "Which is the earnest of our inheritance until the redemption of the purchased possession, unto the praise of his glory." The word for earnest, or the idea of a guarantee, did not really exist in the Swahili language. There is a word for it in the dictionary, which I used, but no one had ever heard of it. When one buys goods at a market stall they don't have any sort of guarantee. The very notion of guarantee does not even exist.

We talked and talked about this and finally one woman said "My husband-to-be gave me a piece of cloth and said that I was to keep it until the day he built a house for us to be together. Would that piece of cloth be a guarantee?"

That was exactly it. I was slowly beginning to understand more and more of how these people lived and thought. Hadn't God promised that 'He would guide me with His eye' and I could see His guidance in so many instances.

I taught the ladies in the mornings and prepared the lessons in the evenings, but I wanted to do something in the afternoons. I did not want my training with CEF to be wasted and so I started praying that I could use it in some way. There was no lack of opportunities, but I wondered where best I could fit it in. Sunday School seemed a good place to begin.

That was only the beginning of another chapter.

8

Bible Study in Bunia

At seven o'clock on Sunday mornings over three hundred boys and girls crowded into Sukisa Church to be taught God's Word. As I helped there it was evident that these children needed to be in classes where teachers would be able to get to know the boys and girls individually.

This would mean teacher-training classes and preparation of materials for the prospective teachers. I realised this was something I could do. There were only five Sunday School teachers, but we knew that we would have to enlist others and enroll them in weekly teacher-training classes. Very soon this teacher-training programme was established.

Sukisa was only one of nine churches in Bunia and soon other pastors were asking that their teachers attend the teacher-training classes. This training was growing bigger than I had ever wanted it to be, but it became evident that this was what the Lord wanted. As a result of those classes hundreds of boys and girls were given a clear presentation of the gospel.

These classes in the various churches brought me into contact with a large cross-section of the local Christian workers. As I got to know the teachers the more it became evident that many of them needed and wanted further teaching. The only way this could be provided was through Bible study groups. This resulted in opening my home each week for a Bible study.

To encourage evangelism we stipulated that anyone planning to attend should bring an unconverted friend who had shown interest in Christianity. Another reason for this stipulation was to eliminate those who just liked attending meetings. Each week over thirty people crowded into my living room and one of our local pastors led the study. My plan was that the meeting would be a training ground for the teachers, but in fact it turned out to be a cultural training and orientation course for me. At those informal meetings I learned many lessons on how the Zairians think and react to certain issues as they freely shared their views.

One most interesting discussion was about inheritance customs, especially when we wandered off into inheritance systems in Zaire. Not only do we have the patriarchal system where the inherited line runs via the male, but also the matriarchal system where the inheritance is passed on via the female. In a matriarchal system where a family has four boys and one girl, only the girl is the beneficiary of the inheritance. I listened intently to one man explain that being from a matriarchal family meant that if he had £10 and both his child and his sister's child were in need, then he was duty bound to pass the gift to his sister's child. The sister came first in family importance and she, and not his child, would carry on the family line as she carried her mother's line. This helped me understand something of the enlarged family unit in Zaire and why many share freely with other Christians in the Church.   As we studied God's Word together we helped each other struggle with many practical issues and in the final analysis we tried to take God at His Word.

Increasing numbers attending the Bunia Theological Seminary made demands on the leadership to increase the capacity for accommodation. Consequently a major building programme was commenced to provide a new chapel and women's classrooms. This gave me opportunity to meet many workers who were employed on the building site. One of these was a young man known as Balagizi. When we had opportunity to discuss Christianity and spiritual matters it became evident that he had very little understanding of what God's Word really taught, but he seemed to be hungry to know more. I invited Balagizi to attend the Bible study group at my home.

Like a blossoming flower responding to warm sunlight, Balagizi's inquiring mind and hungry heart opened to the Scriptures and it was thrilling to watch how God took hold of his life. His marriage was in difficulties at that time and we made this a target for prayer at the group meeting. As we prayed we saw God at work and he and his wife were reunited.

News of this Bible study quickly spread around Bunia and more and more people asked if they could join. One of these was a man who was the deputy leading government official for our area. His wife was a Christian, but he was not and she had urged him to attend the house meeting with her. It was easier for him to visit my house than the residence of one of his fellow countrymen. For him to go to the home of a local Zairian would have been looked upon as favouritism or, even worse, tribalism. He attended the study group regularly and participated well in the discussions. His visits to the Bible study could not be kept secret and when the news circulated that this leading government official was attending our studies it was a good witness in the town. It was especially beneficial that he identified with us for I lived next door to the immigration offices. Being a neighbour to the immigration office meant that I was frequently called upon for many things. They would often come looking for anything from pens or paper to light bulbs.

One Christmas morning two immigration officers arrived at my door. Both were feeling quite unwell and suspected they had malaria which is a common infection in Zaire. The men wanted to know if I could supply them with malarial treatment. Not being a nurse, I had no authority to share medicines with outsiders, but where else would they find anti-malarial medicines on Christmas Day? I was unsure of protocol, but decided I could do nothing else other than let them have the medicine. They were grateful and I wished them well as they went their way. I did not see anything more of them that day, or indeed the next day, which was Sunday. I just hoped they had recovered well from their malaria.

I was having a quiet cup of tea on the Sunday afternoon when a large car pulled up outside the front of my house. It looked like someone important and before they could get to the door I went to meet them. It was then that I recognized the government's Chief Medical Officer for our region and with him the chief political leader for the Bunia area. I welcomed them into the house and after the usual customary greetings the political leader raised the purpose of his visit by saying, "We have a very serious problem in our town and you are the cause of it."

I was shocked beyond belief. What had I done? I had been in Zaire long enough and had sufficient experience to know that problems are best discussed over a cup of tea, so excusing myself I went to the kitchen to collect my thoughts and to make a hurried pot of tea. My thoughts were running riot. *What had I done? What could it be? Will I be expelled from the area?* I tried to review the events of the previous week and the only thing I could think of was the visit of the two immigration officers on Christmas Day. Perhaps that was why the Chief Medical Officer was with the senior Government official. *How would I defend myself? Had they died? I had given medicines to them and was not qualified to do so.* I felt I was in deep trouble and my thoughts ran riot.

Trying to keep my composure, I served the tea while continuing to engage in small talk. I wanted the government official to get to the point, but it took him ages to do so. Finally he broached the subject again saying, "Let me explain the reason for our visit here."

I poised myself to hear every word. "Last Thursday evening a delegation arrived in Bunia from the World Bank. They were here on Friday to meet with the town's leaders and administrators. I personally had a previous engagement and was unable to entertain them on Thursday evening so I called my assistant (his deputy and the government official who was attending our Bible study) and asked him to care for them. He too excused himself saying he had a previous engagement and would be unable to help me. He explained to us that you hold a weekly Bible study here and that he had been learning much about himself, God and God's Word. Our friend also said he was sorry, but for that reason he could not possibly entertain our guests on the night of the study."

As the senior official continued explaining what had happened, he took one deep breath and then, staring at me asked, "Why did you not think it necessary to invite me to this Bible study? Don't you know that I am the number one person in this town and that I need God's Word more than anyone else?"

Turning to the medical officer at his side he added, "And here is our regional doctor. You know what a difficult job he has. He surely needs the help of God's Word too'.

I was flabbergasted. What I had feared was a serious problem was really a blessing. Here was the top political man in our area, which is about the same size as the whole of Ireland, asking if he could come to our Bible study and learn from God's Word.

We spent the next half-hour or so in friendly exchanges during which I cordially invited them to come to the next study. Later when they left my thoughts were in turmoil again. I was praising the Lord for the great opportunity that He had opened to me but was also thinking, "I can't invite all those educated people into this Bible study."

As it was still holiday time I decided I would not move too quickly. Soon my prayer was that the Lord would really show me what I ought to do. I decided that there was no way the first and second citizens of Bunia could be in the same group. The one might intimidate the other. I thought that one way to accommodate both men was to start another Bible study group. To do this I felt we would need other people who were on the same educational level as these men. Prior to the first government official and his wife arriving, those who attended the study were simple people. I now had a predicament as I was not sure where I could find enough educated people who would be interested in Bible study? As I prayed I asked the Lord to send these people across my path.

One man came to my mind. He was a school inspector whom I had met on many previous occasions. One day when I went to purchase diesel for the generators at the Nyankunde hospital, this school inspector was ahead of me in the queue. In Zaire we often had to queue for hours for such commodities. As we waited for an authorising signature in the Petrol Company's office, we chatted about everything. Finally, I decided to mention that I would like to start a Bible study group in my home and asked if he would be interested in coming along.

The inspector proved to be a key person in my predicament. I invited him to come to the same group as the chief political official. During the next three days he came on two occasions to ask if he could invite the customs officials and the airport commander. He really was God's instrument in getting this Bible study started.

It was only weeks later that I discovered that the inspector was a former priest in the Roman Catholic Church, but had decided to marry and had to leave the church. He caused great laughter one night in the Bible study when he said that what he hated most in life was sitting beside older Protestant ladies in church services. He told us that when the preacher announced a reading from a lesser-known book of the Bible such as Amos, even though he had a Bible, he would never attempt to find Amos lest he should be embarrassed in a crowded church. The only places in the Bible he could find were Genesis, Matthew, Mark, Luke and John. However, these older ladies often found Amos very quickly and then would offer to share their Bible with him. He was so embarrassed he would say "Thank you, but I prefer to listen." He then told us how envious he was of those ladies being able to find the difficult books quickly.

Most of the participants in this second Bible study were the elite of Bunia and we were delighted that one of the teachers from Bunia Theological Seminary agreed to lead the studies. The following weeks were weeks of blessings. Not only did the government chief attend, but his wife also came. She was one of the first in the group to trust Jesus Christ as Saviour.

Those who came gained an understanding of God's Word and it took root in their lives. We were all shocked one night when the former priest proclaimed: "What we have seen here tonight is the truth; this is God's Word and we need to obey it in our lives. The rest of you don't look to me like that. You use God's Word just when you want it, but the Bible is something we need to obey daily. I am declaring here tonight that from now I want to follow the Living Word."

The Lord had done a work in the inspector's heart and over the next weeks and months he was like a sponge soaking up whatever teaching he could find in the Scriptures.

There was one man whom I wanted to invite to the Bible study, but I wondered how I could give him the invitation. He was the bank manager and every time I went past the bank, the Lord challenged me to ask him to come to our study. As often as I felt the urge to speak to him I always found some excuses why I should just keep walking past the bank; *I don't have time; I'll come tomorrow; I don't know him very well; What would he think?*

One Friday as I passed by the bank again I made the decision: tomorrow, come rain or shine, I will go into the bank and invite the bank manager to our Bible study. On that Friday afternoon two of our missionaries were leaving and we all went to the airport to say good-bye to them. As we waited for the Missionary Aviation Fellowship plane crowds began to gather at the airport. It was obvious that the national airline had a flight from Kinshasa. Many people were preparing either to leave or to welcome folks arriving. In the middle of the crowd I saw our school inspector and went over to greet him. Soon he introduced me to the bank manager. I could not believe it. My heart was thrilled for I felt this was now my opportunity to invite him to the Bible studies.

As we made small talk I soon discovered he was leaving on the plane. Apparently he had just been transferred to work in Kinshasa. I felt the joy drain from me. I was stunned. I had made so many excuses I had missed my opportunity. How many times I had told the Lord to wait and I will invite the manager tomorrow. My 'tomorrow' never arrived and I was not able to bring this man to our meeting.

I returned to the company of my missionary colleagues and waited for the MAF plane. Tears filled my eyes. The little red and white MAF plane soon arrived and my colleagues boarded it. Tears continued to trickle down my face. One of my friends turned to me and said, "I didn't know you were such a close friend with these missionaries." I made no reply. I couldn't tell her that the real reason for my tears was a missed opportunity to share God's Word with someone the Lord had laid on my heart. I was devastated.

The Lord was gracious to me and I have proved so many times He knows our needs and sends His grace just in the nick of time. Next morning the school inspector arrived at my home. He brought with him a visitor. It was the new bank manager who was a Christian. He came to say he would love to attend our Bible study. Months later I sat enthralled in our Bible study group when this new bank manager brought greetings from the former bank manager and wanted all who knew him to know that he had just become a Christian in Kinshasa.

It taught me that God can do His work without us, but He loves us to be involved in His wonderful plan for the salvation of men and women. I had missed out on one blessing, but it was still a blessing to know that my failure and missed opportunity had not frustrated God's plan.

9

Government Officials and the Gospel

Governments are the same the world over. They all need money to function. In some countries the officials also seem to need some extra cash and they often put pressure on the people to pay up. I was soon to learn that Africa was no exception. It certainly was impossible to avoid contact with these officials in Zaire.

I had only been in Bunia a few weeks when I needed to apply for my driving licence. Colleagues assured me it would take a long time and many weary visits to the police office to convince them that I had paid the official fee and that that was all I was prepared to pay. In my home area of Broughshane people have a reputation for being somewhat frugal and I certainly was not disposed to giving more money than I thought I should, so I duly went to the office, completed all the application forms and paid my fee. Now I would wait, with my heels dug in. Some told me I could wait months, but it was not to be so.

Early one Sunday I joined with others to attend a service in the newly-formed French church at the Theological Seminary. We had invited various people to this new service and were sure the educated people would appreciate it. All of the church services had previously been in Swahili, but with more government officials in the town, we felt it would be a good outreach to conduct a service in French, which is the official language of the country.

It was a particularly hot Sunday morning and the preacher went on a little longer than usual. The classroom at the seminary where the service was conducted was packed to capacity. Finally, the closing hymn was announced and we all stood to sing praise to the Lord. One member of the congregation, seated in front of Shirley and myself, was overcome with the heat and fainted. At the time, I was new in the area and was not sure what to do. I suggested to my colleague that we should open the collar of his shirt and put his head between his knees. She quickly replied, "We'll do it? No, no! You do it."

I stepped forward to help the man and soon he was conscious again. We helped him into Shirley's little VW Beetle and drove him to his home. By the time we arrived there the man had completely recovered.

On Monday evening we decided to call by his home again and see if he was well. We arrived to find him fit and well and he insisted that we go in for a chat. In conversation we soon discovered he was the principal man who was responsible for issuing driving licences in Bunia. I had mine the next day. I really was assured that the Lord was looking after me.

While teaching at the school for women in the Bunia Theological Seminary I began to understand many of the difficulties these ladies face in Zaire. One great problem they are confronted with is providing sufficient clothing for their families. With this in mind we turned the practical classes into time for sewing, knitting and crocheting. However, there was difficulty in obtaining materials with which they could make shirts, shorts, skirts and other garments. In the knitting classes we knit vests and bonnets, but wool was so expensive and we were very limited in our budget. We looked upon the need for clothes as a necessity so we made it a matter of prayer. In the meantime we struggled along with great difficulty.

During my first furlough in Northern Ireland I happened to mention to a friend that if she had any wool left over after knitting her jumpers, I could use it in Zaire. This lady not only kept balls of wool for us, but she told all her friends that Maizie Smyth needed wool. As a result we had wool, wool and more wool, of all grades and colours. There was so much wool I had to use some as packing to insulate the barrels, which were being shipped to Zaire. With the wool that was left over I filled seven large potato sacks and sent them via surface mail to Zaire.

Months later when I returned to Zaire there was still no sign of the sacks arriving in the mail. The Post Office was notorious for extracting small fines from us. We suspected they had learned from the officials at other government departments that these people were good for a few extra dollars. They often told us, "This packet has been here one week and you have to pay depot charges." or "This letter does not have the correct address so you must pay a fine." and even, "This is not a letter, but a small packet so you must pay a handling charge." Month after month passed and there was no sign of the wool arriving. I eventually was dreading the day that my seven sacks of wool would arrive in the mail. They eventually arrived in Bunia more than one year after posting them in Ireland.

I was called to the Post Office and told that I must pay customs on these imported goods. The Customs official duly arrived and even though I tried to assure him that I had packed the wool and there was nothing else in the bag, he ordered me to open a sack. He said, "Please empty the bag on to the floor."

I upended the sack and out spilled balls of wool in every direction. The sober-faced official was not impressed and told me to open the second sack. I did as I was told and again the wool went in every direction. By this time there were balls of wool everywhere and what a job I had trying to gather them up and put them back into the sacks. When I had gathered up the wool and closed the two sacks the man pointed to the third sack and asked me to open it also. Reluctantly, and with a lot of protests, I opened up the third potato bag. I tried to explain to the official what the wool was for and that I had packed it myself. I assured him again there was nothing else in any of the sacks, but he ignored my protests and insisted that I open the fourth sack. By this time I was not very happy at this routine, but he was the government official and I had to do what I was told. I took my time and slowly packed up the third sack before emptying the fourth onto the floor.

As the balls of wool scattered across the room the official suddenly took a dive into the middle of them and lifted up a ball of grey wool. "That's it. That's it!" he repeated excitedly.

I looked at him in amazement and wondered what he had found or what he thought the grey wool was. His faced changed and with a broad grin he went on to explain that he had a grey pullover at home with a hole in it and was looking for the right colour of wool to darn it. He told me to pack up the rest of my wool and take it home. I had no customs to pay and he went home a happy man.

So often we say that God has the right man at the right place at the right time to accomplish His purpose. I had already proved this on these two occasions, but there was more proof to follow. Our new house in Bunia was on the corner of a main road and at the top of a hill. When the main water piping was installed originally, they directed the water along the hill and around a corner for the water to flow downhill. It was on this downhill pipe from which they branched the water into our house, but because the water rushed downward, there was very little water pressure to give us any supply. This meant we were constantly without water.

I am not sure why the other missionaries delegated me to go and see the head of the water service. Perhaps they thought I had more forthrightness than charm and a little forthrightness was now needed. I asked if we could have the intake pipe enter the house from the other side on the level ground at the top of the hill. The official to whom I spoke was sympathetic to my request and he and his financial advisor told me how much we would have to pay. It was not a large amount and so the deal was settled on the spot. Later that day I was able to buy the materials we would need and all was put in place for work to begin the following morning.

No workers turned up next morning at the given hour, but that was not unusual so we patiently waited. By lunchtime rumours were rife around town that the head official at the water office, the man with whom I had spoken and done the deal, had absconded with all the money from the coffers. I panicked. *What would happen now? Had we lost everything? When would our job be done?*

Several weeks went by and nothing happened. The metal pipes were rusting in our garage. At length I felt it was time to return to the water office and negotiate another deal with the new chief of the water service. I wondered if he would honour the commitment made by his predecessor. When I arrived there I was surprised to discover that a Christian man had been appointed as the new administrator and he assured me he would send the workmen to do the work.

Weeks went by and still nothing happened until one day the workmen arrived unexpectedly at our home and within a few hours they connected us up for a better water supply. I recollected how the Lord had worked this out for us. If we had not signed the deal with the former chief at the water office we never would have had a good supply of water in our house. Truly the Lord had guided us at the right time, to the right place and the right person to help us.

The Missionary Aviation Fellowship flew in and out of Bunia frequently. Not all of the passengers were necessarily missionaries. Part of my ministry was to help the MAF pilot and his passengers. This opened up all kinds of doors of opportunity with government employees who came and went. Day after day I was dealing with immigration and customs officials. I was able to build lasting friendships with many of these officials and even to this day they continue to help our ministry in Zaire. However, at times they also had their financial difficulties in trying to make ends meet, especially coming near the end of the month. For many of them I was a very present help in time of debt, a place where they could obtain a small loan to tide them over.

They knew they had to repay me or they couldn't ask me again next month. Of course there were the usual requests when leaving on furlough like, "Please look for a watch for my wife." For others it might be sunglasses or some other luxury item. One man worked with me in Zaire for many years, but never asked for anything and was most helpful. One day, near to the date of departure for furlough, I was on my way home from the airport when he asked me if I could help him when I got back into town. Although he had never asked me for anything before I was sure he was going to ask me to bring him a watch or some other item.

I mulled it over in my mind and when we arrived in the centre of town I was ready for him. I waited for a few minutes and then asked what it was he wanted. It looked like he had been trying to muster up the courage to make his request, so hesitatingly he said, "Please tell me how I can trust in Jesus." You can imagine my complete shock. I was amazed, but also very excited and we spent the next half-hour or so sharing from the Scriptures how he could trust the Saviour.

In the few remaining weeks in Bunia before I left for furlough it was great to see that man attend our Bible studies and soon afterwards become involved in Christian work. He left Bunia shortly after my departure, but over the years I have met him in various places and it is wonderful to see him continuing to live and witness for the Lord.

The airport at Bunia was not very busy. Only about ten flights came in and went out each week. This meant that the airport workers had plenty of free time on their hands. Although there had been a great drive in Zaire to promote literacy, there was a tremendous lack of reading material. It was great to receive from Every Home Crusade in Belfast, very good evangelical literature, which I was able to distribute to these workers. Besides benefiting from reading the literature individually, we were able join with them for several question and answer sessions while we waited for various planes to arrive. Eventually we were able to offer Bibles to the airport staff, and these were gladly accepted. Many of these workers came to our Bible studies and several of them trusted the Saviour.

During the Bible studies it became evident that the airport workers were studying the Bible passages before coming to the Bible study and were therefore asking very intelligent questions. This hunger for God's Word brought us great joy. One young fellow who had been living with his girl friend for over a year announced he could not continue to live with her any more until he was married. It was clear that God's Word was touching every area of their lives.

The airport commander also joined the study group for the government officials and he trusted the Lord Jesus at that group. Ten years later I met him at another airport where he informed me that at the evening school, he had just completed classes in evangelism and was now an elder in his local church where he also headed up the church's evangelistic programme. In heaven we will be able to understand where all the seedlings from that Bible study sprouted for the Lord.

10

Expatriates in Bunia

Bunia was the commercial centre for Zaire's Ituri region and many Greeks and Indians had opened shops in the town. Their businesses helped bring a lot of needed finance and development to Bunia. However, one of the big disadvantages we faced was the lack of building supplies, which were not easily obtained. Most building materials needed in Bunia were imported from Kenya or Uganda and came by road. This process frequently involved a lot of delays and sometimes an order could take weeks to arrive in Bunia. With no telephone link to Kenya or Uganda there was no way to place an order or ascertain if, and when, an order might have been dispatched. This meant we had to endure in painful silence and with much patience.

We always enjoyed visiting the Greek and Indian shops. Besides the welcome bargains or novelties we might find, we also shared news with these expatriates of what was happening elsewhere in the world. News in Zaire tended to be local news, what was happening in Zaire or a few other neighbouring countries. Perhaps that was because there was enough trouble happening in Zaire and the nearby states to fill any news bulletin. When we heard titbits of news or even rumours we usually asked on which radio station it was heard. Local gossip was often referred to as 'the footpath radio' or the 'radio without batteries.'

Most of the Greeks belonged to the Greek Orthodox Church and often celebrated 'an official day'. On that day they choose the name of one of their saints and gave a small reception at their home in the saint's honour. We were usually invited along to these receptions which were great social occasions. Besides it being an opportunity to taste different cuisine, it was also an opening to build bridges of friendship, although I would not say that swallowing the specialty of liver soup with raw egg was my favourite way of making new friends.

At their homes it was always a problem to know at what stage the meal would be served. I remember on one occasion we had a fish dish after the soup and then some crepes with a mince steak filling. I was sure this was the main course so I heartily tucked into two of these delicious crepes. I was horrified when the steak and chips were served immediately after the crepes. Hot peppers and chillies garnished each dish and the mince was particularly hot. I attempted to cool down my mouth with a baby tomato, but then I almost collapsed. I didn't know that the cook had hidden chilli in the tomato and when it burst in my mouth I thought I was on fire.

These informal meetings with the Greeks gave opportunities to share in their times of family problems and sorrows. When they were sick we were often called to help, give advice or to make radio contact with the doctors at Nyankunde Mission Hospital. The hospital was set up by five different mission boards in the 1960s and had a good reputation in the region. This was mainly due to the work of Dr. Becker and Dr. Helen Roseveare. Dr. Kyle, a UFM missionary from Derriaghy near Belfast, for whom I had prayed for many years since my 'Presbyterian Hostel' days, was the hospital Director after Dr. Becker retired. Their good reputation went before them and many national doctors joined the hospital because of its prestigious renown. Most business families in Bunia, expatriates and many locals often made the forty-five kilometre journey from Bunia to Nyankunde to be treated there.

Early one Saturday morning one of the Greeks came to my home and asked me what they should do about their baby daughter who had cried most of the night. The man was understandably distraught for she was their only daughter and just a few months old. As we chatted I thought it would be best for them to drive the baby to the hospital at Nyankunde. They wrapped the infant in some blankets and with their three boys the whole family sped off to Nyankunde in their car.

At lunchtime a radio call came through asking for prayer for the little girl who was very seriously ill. There was no radio link on Sunday and we had no further news until early on Monday. The news was not good. The little girl had died during the night. Soon I was called to the home and for the next three days I spent a lot of time with the family and other Greek friends we had come to know and respect in Bunia. The little girl's mother was heartbroken and on many occasions during the weeks that followed the bereavement she would ask me to pray with her.

During one of these visits in which I prayed with the family, I took the opportunity to pass on Christian literature in the Greek language. The little girl's death opened many doors for us to share our faith with our Greek friends.

Atul, an Indian businessman, had moved into town and his prices seemed very reasonable. When any new shop opened in a small town like Bunia we always paid a visit to see what was on offer. We found the prices at this new shop very competitive so we decided to buy some of our supplies for the Bible Schools and Mission work from Atul.

One day Atul said to me that I had never gone to greet his wife, Kishori, who loved to speak English. I started visiting their home and found Kishori to be a very friendly person. We continued to buy goods in Atul's shop and had many opportunities to speak to him about spiritual matters. These opportunities opened the door for me to give Atul another Bible for he had lost the first one I gave him.

Atul only agreed to accept the Bible if I would take a copy of the Holy Geeta, which is the Hindu holy book. I took the Geeta but I never read it; however, in less than two months he had read most of the Bible. His brother also became interested and soon I was having a simple Bible study for their family. They had many questions, but one of their greatest fears was that their mother might see them reading an English Bible. She would only receive something that was in their native Gujarati language, but I did not have a Gujarati Bible.

The MAF plane came from Nairobi the next day and to my surprise the pilot was John Miller who had been with me at B.T.I. in Glasgow. I had seen him about three times in the previous six years, but God arranged for him to be on that flight that very day to help me. I asked John if Gujarati Bibles were available in Nairobi as I would like one for Atul's mother.

On the next flight from Nairobi to Bunia John sent me a Gujarati Bible, which solved the mother's problem. Often Atul asked questions such as; "How do I know God sees me?" "How do I know God hears me?" "How can I be sure that Jesus is the way to heaven?" "What difference is there between Jesus and my Hindu gods?" Many hours were spent in discussions.

News that Atul and his brother were reading God's Word soon got to the ears of the local Moslems in Bunia. They were not happy and did everything to try and swing Atul's searching mind in their direction. They gave him videos, which featured a debate between a Moslem and a Christian, in which the Moslem tried to prove that Jesus did not really die on the cross. The more Islamic material they gave him the more Atul kept reading the Scriptures and we also kept praying for him. One night each week these Indian families came to my home for a Bible study together with the Christian bank manager. They posed many difficult questions and to be truthful I had to leave some of them unanswered.

It was during this time that one of Atul's brothers-in-law came to visit the family in Bunia. I found the brother-in-law stranded at the airport without a means of transport into the town, which was nearly six kilometres away. I gave him a ride and on the way he asked me why I was in Bunia. This opened an opportunity for me to share with him what Jesus Christ had done in my life and why I was in Zaire. I dropped him off at Atul's house and went on my way.

Shortly after the brother-in-law's visit I left for furlough, but before leaving I gave some literature to Atul and his brother to read and study while I was out of the country. During my time back in Broughshane I continued to pray for these two brothers. With no telephone or fax system available at their end I had very little news of them.

Many months later while I was still in Ireland I received the good news that both Atul and his brother had trusted the Lord Jesus Christ when they went on a family visit to India. When I returned to Bunia I went to Atul's shop at the first opportunity. The counter staff had changed and so I just asked an assistant if I could speak with Atul. This Indian man looked up and quickly ran around the counter to hug me. I stared at him in disbelief. I had never seen this man before, but he obviously had no doubt who I was. I stood there as stiff as a poker, dumbfounded and absolutely sure the man had made an embarrassing mistake. *Who is he?* I muttered to myself.

Undeterred by my lack of reaction the stranger looked me in the eye and said, "Thank you for being the first person to tell me about Jesus. Remember you gave me a ride from the airport to Atul's house one day last year. Now I am your brother in Christ."

I was awestruck and my heart leaped for joy at this great news that Atul's brother-in-law had become a Christian. God had done far more for him than I had ever asked or even imagined He would do. God took hold of Atul's family and greatly used him.

Later Atul completed a Bible School course; his brother directs a Christian video production company, a printing press and recently produced an Indian edition of the Jesus video. These men have been a great Christian witness to their extended family and I know of fifteen other relations who have come to know the Lord Jesus Christ as Saviour because of them.

Not only did the family see the difference the Lord Jesus had made in their lives, but so too did the business community in Zaire with whom they worked. Shortly after Atul trusted the Lord a large tobacco company approached him and asked for his projected sales for the following year. They were congratulating him that during that year his business had been their best sales outlet for that whole region of Zaire. The company representative told Atul to take his time to complete the projected sales form. Atul told them he could fill in the details immediately for he knew to the last cigarette how many he would sell during the following year. The representative joked and said, "You know a lot of things, but I bet you don't know the exact number you will sell."

Atul wasn't laughing when he assured the man he did. The representative looked at Atul writing the projected figure for tobacco sales for the incoming year. The representative could not believe what he saw for after every question Atul wrote "ZERO, ZERO, ZERO, ZERO."

Atul then went on to tell the man how Jesus had changed his life and he could not sell cigarettes to destroy other lives. Atul's business dealings were the talk of the town. He paid full customs duties on all goods he imported and refused to traffic in any sort of bribery. He also became very publicly involved in the local church in Bunia. God certainly transformed these lives.

Over the years I have maintained contact with Atul and his family. When they opened a shop in Kisangani I shared fellowship with one of Atul's brothers, Nilesh, who managed the shop and many happy evenings were spent at their home. It was a special joy to see Nilesh's wife really take her stand for God at the baptism service in the River Congo when she publicly professed faith in Christ.

God did a special work in their lives and both in Bunia and Kisangani they exemplify the biblical truth that God will honour those who honour Him. I never thought that giving a Bible to someone would have such long-term results and God is still working through them.

11

Sifu Sifu and Sunday School

After teaching at the Women's Bible School at the Bunia Theological Seminary for two years, the Seminary board asked me to consider becoming the Director of the Women's Bible School. I thought and prayed about the responsibility and felt constrained to accept the position. Being Director provided me with many challenges. Most of the ladies were married to pastors and I had a great desire to see them trained as competent wives and assets to their husband's ministry after they graduated. Some ladies came to us with secondary education whilst others had never been to school. Literacy classes were set up, but often the most difficult battle was convincing a husband of the importance that his wife should learn to read and write. Frequently the husband was content for his spouse to be a 'housewife' and care for his children. Sometimes the pastor objected because, when his wife went to study, he had added family responsibilities.

At the Women's Bible School we tried to place more emphasis on practical ministry rather than classroom theory. Each year we targeted a section of the community for our outreach. Five-day clubs and helping Sunday Schools were highlighted one year. Because I taught Child Evangelism classes I became very heavily involved in this practical work.

We arranged a Five-day club at Sukisa, the largest local church at that time in Bunia. There seemed to be a great spiritual hunger in the hearts of the children. Each afternoon increasing numbers of boys and girls crowded into the church and listened attentively to God's Word. Typical of the interest created among these little ones were three children from one family who finished school each day just after midday. Instead of walking one mile to their home they waited three hours for the club to begin. One of them, a ten-year-old girl, trusted the Saviour during that week.

Our chief objective in the Five-day club was to reach the unchurched children of Bunia with the gospel, so when we saw the church filled each day and listened to their happy voices singing the praises of our Saviour we were delighted. Because memorisation played a big part in school education in Zaire it seemed easy for them to learn their memory verses.

Sunday School was the ideal place to follow up those who had trusted the Saviour during the week. That ten-year-old girl never came to the Sunday School so I went to visit her. At her home I discovered that her mother had been very ill for a couple of weeks and therefore the young daughter had to stay home to cook the dinner and do the housework. I was invited in and was able to share God's Word with them. The mother was lying on a grass mat on the floor, but she made room for us to share her mat. Her other small children gathered round and jostled with each other to sit near the white woman visitor. The little room was now full to overflowing. When father appeared the children scattered and provided a prominent place in the middle of the room where he relaxed into his deck chair.

By this time we had started singing choruses and quoting the memory verses we had learned the previous week. An impromptu quiz was arranged to see if anything had really been understood from the last week's teaching. The chorus singing and the Bible lessons captivated Mum and Dad. As we continued to sing and exchange Bible truths the crowd grew. Many of these children had never heard a white woman speak Swahili before and perhaps that was one of the factors that drew so many to this simple house.

So great was the crowd outside that soon the door was blocked and the room darkened by people peering in through the small windows. Besides the dark shadows, the children outside created such a racket that it became almost impossible to make ourselves heard. The father finally concluded that the room was too dark and full and suggested we move outside to teach everyone. That was the first step in initiating an open air Sunday School that continued for many years in that predominantly Roman Catholic part of town.

As part of their training some ladies from the Bible School joined with me every Sunday afternoon to hold a Bible club in front of that house. Often the neighbours would come and listen to God's Word. Through our teaching programme at least one neighbour trusted Jesus Christ as her Saviour and some children came to know the Saviour too.

The family, in whose yard we held the club, continued to have many health problems. One day the mother, Wele, came in great distress to see me. She said her brother had left the previous evening for a three-day fishing trip to Lake Albert, which was about sixty kilometres away. His heavily pregnant wife was left at home to care for the children, one of whom had become very ill. At first they thought it was malaria which was very common in Zaire. That night, following the husband's departure, the wife had gone into labour. Sadly, during the confinement she haemorrhaged to death, but the newborn baby survived. Wele, was at her wit's end, and understandably so, for she had a newborn niece on her hands, her sister-in-law was dead, a little nephew was critically ill and his father away from home for three days.

As is customary, the funeral had to be held on the same day. Lack of communication meant that the father would not learn the news of his wife's death for at least another day. The family all pulled together to buy a coffin, dig a grave and arrange a funeral service. They decided to conduct the funeral service at the same spot where we operated our weekly Sunday School. I remember we were half way through the funeral service when a lady came running. As she got nearer to us, her wails and shrieks got louder. Wele went to meet her hoping to calm her down a little, but soon she was crying too. The poor woman was on her way to let us know that the sick child, who was suspected of having had malaria, had just passed away. We were all stunned. How could I help in such a situation? I clearly remember sitting there that afternoon and thinking, *Will I ever understand why these things are allowed to happen?*

I had many opportunities in the following days to share in that home. The saddest moment was when the father arrived from his trip to find his wife and son had both died and were already buried. His plight was further complicated by the fact that he had a newborn baby to care for. It was an unforgettable experience for many of the ladies from the Bible School and gave them an insight to the problems that their husbands might encounter during their pastoral ministry.

We were forced into opening a second Sunday School in a most unusual way. On another Sunday afternoon we returned to the same clearing for our weekly Bible club only to discover that Wele had moved house during the week. There was no problem holding a Bible Club for most of the neighbours were waiting for us and invited us to use their yard. The Lord kept that door open for quite a while and we so much enjoyed teaching those children the Word of God. It was especially good for me to be in touch with the children and keep up with their thinking. This helped greatly as I continued to teach the Child Evangelism classes at the Bible School.

Week after week we congregated in one of those dusty yards. The afternoon sun was hot and with no shade it beat down upon us. The humid atmosphere and perspiration added to the discomfort, making our clothes stick to us. The usual noises of village life blended with our singing. I am not blessed with a good singing voice so we tended to stick to the same few choruses that I knew well. In Zaire choruses were not well known so many of the women only learned them as we went along.

A favourite chorus with the children was "Praise Him, Praise Him, our loving Lord." We sang it week after week and even the ladies often hummed the music as we travelled. The word for *praise* in Swahili is *sifu*. Before I knew it the children were calling me "Sifu Sifu". I wish I could say that I gained that name because I was always praising God. It seems I earned the nickname "Sifu" because I had sung the chorus every week for months. The children loved the chorus and enjoyed the fun also. The name stuck.

Three weeks had passed since we moved to this neighbour's yard and all seemed fine. One Tuesday evening I heard someone at my door and when I answered, there stood Wele. She was not in very good form and after the formal greetings started to talk to me with quite a forceful voice. "Is it true that because I moved house my children don't need to be taught God's Word?" she asked in no uncertain terms.

I tried to explain that I did not know her new location, but was quite willing to go to her new home for a Bible club after we taught the first class on a Sunday afternoon. I did not know what the women at the Bible School would think for I had planned two Bible clubs that afternoon instead of one. After explaining to me where her new house was Wele looked straight into my eye and said, "You know that there are far more children there than were at the original place." Over a cup of tea she continued, "Do you not have a responsibility to teach them too?"

What could I say? There was no way I could refuse her, so very soon several willing ladies joined me every Sunday afternoon to conduct the two open air Sunday Schools. The second location proved to have many more children just as the lady had said. At least one hundred attended each week and many boys and girls came to know the Lord at that Bible club.

I was embarrassed when I found out that in the area I was known to many parents as "Sifu Sifu." Each week we would make the three-mile round trip just to reach these children for the Lord. There was a good local church nearby and so the children were channelled into the morning Sunday School there. The local pastor and church members were very grateful for more children attending their church and some of the Sunday School teachers decided to join with us for the afternoon class. These teachers attended our Teacher Training Course each week and they continued to teach and reach boys and girls for the Saviour.

God blessed us in teaching His Word to many of those children. I may never see any of those boys and girls again on earth, but hopefully I will see many of them among that great multitude in heaven singing "Salvation belongs to our God, who sits on the throne and to the Lamb."

One day during this time I was making my way by Land Rover to a conference on the other side of Bunia. My vehicle was full of pastors who had come from many far-flung villages in the bush. These were mainly Bible School teachers who had come to attend a meeting in which they would plan future courses for the Bible School students. As we rumbled along we came to a place where the police were doing a spot check on the road. Often when the police stop a vehicle it means they are hungry or are looking for money. If they find a motorist does not have his papers in order these policemen can really be extortionate.

I knew all my papers were in order so while two young policemen questioned the drivers in front I waited patiently. When my turn came, one of the young guards began to question me also. Just then I heard someone shout with a loud voice "That's Sifu Sifu. Let her through. Her papers are in order."

That other police officer who called out was the father of one of the young people who attended our Bible club and whose house was right beside where we taught our lessons. He frequently sat in the shade of his own yard on a Sunday afternoon listening to God's Word.

Through three young children waiting after school the Lord had opened impossible doors for us to sow His Word week by week in those two Bible clubs.

12

The Highs and Lows of Campus Life

The daily routine of preparing and teaching classes, attending to the School's administration and heading up its programme in Bunia, kept me in contact with many students. Besides showing interest and involvement in their work I found that many of them lowered their guard and began to unburden to me about their family life.

A student who was several months pregnant believed that she should not eat fish or meat during her pregnancy. Their tribal custom imposed a milk-only diet during pregnancy. In Bunia she could not find enough milk and even if she had, her family could not have afforded to purchase it. We made arrangements with the hospital at Nyankunde that they would conduct 'well-mother-and-baby' clinics monthly at our school. Ladies of our surrounding area were invited to attend.

One evening, after the clinic had finished, a male nurse came to me. He was in some distress and told me that the pregnant student who had shared her dilemma with me would deliver a dead child unless she started to eat some protein. We discussed how this was possible in view of their tribal customs. In the exchange the nurse left with this word, "I've told you about it and now it is up to you to do something."

I was annoyed at this male nurse and his attitude to the mother and me, but what could I say? I pondered what I could do to help the mother-to-be. I knew she was also opposed to eating eggs, but to me that seemed the only route available. My training on the Broughshane farm had not left me and at the rear of the house I kept chickens to provide fresh eggs. Each day I mixed two raw eggs with milk and some other flavour to disguise the taste and took them with me to school. I told the student, "This is the medicine the nurse says you must drink." Of course, this was true for the nurse had told me the girl needed protein.

The pregnant student took my concoction each day for the next few months. One morning her husband arrived at the classroom to tell us that his wife had just gone in to labour and had been admitted to the maternity clinic across town. Two hours later he returned with the news that his wife had delivered a healthy baby girl. He said to me, "As you have provided so much medicine for her we would like to give you the honour of naming our child."

I told the happy father I would think about it and soon let him know the name I had chosen. Choosing names for newborns was something that I had to do quite frequently and I always tried to provide a name that would bring honour to God. I tried to make them simple enough too as they had to live with it for the rest of their lives. The students had obviously heard the father asking me to choose a name and so at break time they decided I needed some help. I had not confided in anyone what 'the medicine' was, but at break-time two of the more astute ladies came to me. Their eyes were dancing when they mischievously said, "We suggest you call the child Egg"

I settled on calling the little child Joy. The episode taught me that no one has any secrets in Zaire.

Living near church headquarters meant sharing a lot of hospitality with church visitors and especially at the annual church committee meetings. Extra help was always needed in the kitchen in the evening and it was usually the male students from the Bible School who would be invited to provide the help.

Following a meal for between fifteen to twenty committee members, it was very common to hear the students go through a 'revision test' while they washed dishes in the kitchen. Of course, the students had their meal too and then whatever was left over was taken home to their families. Understandably the students enjoyed being invited and long before the proposed committee meetings they would be offering their services. During the week they had revision in the kitchen, a free meal, money for the pleasure of being there and take-home meals for the family. Many church leaders still jokingly say, "A qualification for being a church leader in Zaire is to have washed dishes at Maizie's sink."

Most of the students travel hundreds of kilometres from their homes to be at Bunia and contact with their sending churches is often very limited. This is particularly difficult when they need financial help from their home churches. Students in Zaire are usually abandoned by the churches to 'fend for themselves' during their three years in Bunia. We therefore try to provide work for the less well-off students and what better place than in the missionary's home or garden. In Zaire I have always been blessed to have a house with a large garden. There was enough land to plant corn, beans, bananas and tomatoes. Much of the labour to maintain this was provided by the students who were paid for their work. I also had to pay them to harvest the crops and they usually ended up taking much of the produce home to their families.

One family, who came over three hundred kilometres to be at the Bible College, seemed to be anxious to find work. Early one Saturday morning Kokyakake, the husband, came to my home and said, "I just want to say thank you for the way you have helped us. I want to work today, but I won't take any pay for it." He was a first year student and had helped Shirley and me move to a new location. There was plenty of work to be done and we were encouraged by this student's lovely attitude, especially from someone who knew we missionaries could afford to pay what he would earn and this would augment his meagre budget. We were touched that he just wanted to work to say "Thank you".

A short time later an epidemic of cholera struck Bunia and Kokyakake's child was one of the first children to fall victim to it. The young boy was transferred the forty-five kilometres to the Mission Hospital at Nyankunde. The staff fought for the life of that little boy, but it was in vain. The student body gathered round that grief-stricken family when they laid their darling son to rest on a Friday afternoon. So many of them had experienced loss through death in their own families and knew something of what Kokyakake and his wife were experiencing. We prayed that the Lord would help them through the trying days and give them the courage to continue to cope with pressures of Bible College.

The weekend brought welcome respite to the young couple and provided some days to recover from their grief before Monday's classes, which they wanted to attend. However, Sunday brought them more discouraging news. Kokyakake's wife became unwell and soon we knew that she too had cholera. We had to take her immediately to the Nyankunde hospital where she was cared for by capable Christian hands. Meanwhile, our hearts were broken as we cried out to the Lord to restore her to health and to her husband, Kokyakake.

Monday passed with no good news and so on Tuesday after classes I made the trip to Nyankunde hospital to visit with them. When I got there she was lying motionless on a mat because the beds were all taken as the cholera epidemic swept the area. There were cholera victims in beds, others beside or under the beds, some on mats in the corridors or wherever they could find a space to lie down. It was horrific. Our sadness was compounded when we learned that there was little hope for Kokyakake's wife. After my visit and prayer Kokyakake walked the short distance with me from the hospital to the Land Rover. Broken in every way, through his tears he said, "I believed God called my wife and myself to serve Him together. Now it looks as though He is taking my wife home to Himself? Have I got it all wrong?"

He was a broken man and I was broken too. Having lost his son the previous week, now he had little hope that his wife would survive. What could one say? I wanted to tell Him that God's plans are always for the best, but that was not what he wanted to hear at that moment. I assured him that at the school we would be praying specially for him and his wife and whatever route God was choosing for them. I tried to assure him that God would give them the grace to walk with Him.

On arriving back at the Bible School I called all the women together and we spent quite a time praying for our dear sister. We asked that the Lord would restore her to health again. We were totally cast upon the Lord and felt inadequate. A call from the hospital early the next morning filled me with fear. Initially I thought I would have to make the trip to Nyankunde to pick up a corpse. No. The call was from the doctor telling me that there had been such a change in our student overnight and she was now taking fluids. Things certainly looked a lot better. She continued to progress and in a few days joined us again at school. The Lord had heard our prayers yet again and we praised Him for all that He had done for her. It was a great day when we welcomed her back to our classroom.

I continued to take a particular interest in Kokyakake and his wife and their little family and it was amazing to see the Lord lead them in His Way. While they were still at Bunia, God gave them a great burden to reach Muslims with the gospel. Today they serve the Lord as the first Congolese missionaries to Chad where they are reaching Muslims for Christ.

It is not easy to continually cope with so much sickness and death. At Bunia we always seemed to be dealing with crisis situations and this made us depend on the Lord more to guide us in what was best to do. One church, which had heard of the Bunia Theological College, but had never sent students to it, decided to send three of their best couples. One of them had travelled many hundreds of kilometres to be at Bible School. The couple had been married for quite a few years, but were childless. They had been praying for years that the Lord would give them a family. They were very much in love with each other and knew the Lord had brought them together. They were also content for whatever His will might be for them. They knew the Lord would guide and provide.

You can imagine how overjoyed they were when they discovered she was carrying a child and although dogged by sickness for the nine months, she delivered a very healthy baby boy. He was their pride and joy and all the Bible School family shared their happiness. We felt that we all had prayed for this child. The happy couple lovingly cared for their new baby, but when he was eight months old he became very sick and had to be transferred to the Mission Hospital at Nyankunde. All efforts made to save the baby's life were in vain. It was not only a bitter blow to the young couple who had so loved their baby, but to us all who had shared in their joy and grief. It was a very sad day at Bunia when we laid that little body to rest.

During the weeks that followed we tried to comfort the distraught couple. Sometimes we read Job's words too readily; "The Lord gave and the Lord hath taken away; blessed be the name of the Lord." It is one thing to read these words in the comfort of health and strength, but the words take on another meaning standing beside an empty crib or at an open grave holding a grief-stricken mother as the thuds of red clay fall on top of her baby's casket. We still believe God is in control of every situation and makes no mistakes.

The next few months were difficult as we continued to pray for that family. We surrounded them with our love and prayers. God was gracious to them and nearly two years later they welcomed another little life into their family.

Transferring the sick children from Bunia to Nyankunde was not without its difficulties, especially in the rainy season. One couple at the Bunia College, whose young child suffered from sickle-cell anaemia, had to travel to the Nyankunde hospital almost every month for blood transfusions. It was not always possible to go by road. Once during the wet season it had been raining heavily for a couple of days and the four-year-old boy had obviously got a chill in the wet weather even though his mother had tried to keep him warm and dry. The early morning examination at the Bible School dispensary revealed he was on the threshold of another crisis and should be transferred to the hospital immediately. He needed blood within two hours to avoid a serious crisis. To travel to Nyankunde by road would have been impossible. On the wet slippery road it would take at least two or three hours besides being soaked in the pouring rain.

I knew that MAF was due to arrive in Bunia on the way to Nyankunde in their small five-seater plane. Perhaps they would have a place for the mother and child. We waited at the airport for ten minutes hoping the plane would arrive in good time to help the stricken boy. It did arrive within a short time and we were pleased to see a passenger disembark in Bunia. That meant there would be a place for the mother. Our hopes were dashed when we heard the place was already reserved for a passenger connecting with an international flight. *What could we do now?* I thought to myself.

Paul Brown, one of my missionary colleagues, was on the plane and he suggested that he could take the child in his arms to Nyankunde and, while they refuelled the plane there, he would call for the hospital taxi to take the sick infant to the hospital. It seemed to be the only way to ensure this little boy would arrive at the hospital before it was too late. The mother flatly refused to let her boy go. What a dilemma! To keep the child in Bunia was sentencing him to a certain death, but if the mother trusted her boy to the care of my missionary colleague there was the possibility of survival. Urgent prayers went up to heaven asking for an immediate answer. "Lord what is the best we can do? What should we do?"

The mother could not be persuaded and so I decided to use my clout as 'school headmistress' and with an air of authority commanded her to let the child go before it was too late. We contacted the hospital and they said they would send a taxi to meet the child at the airport and begin the treatment immediately. We assured the mother that she could follow by road. She finally consented, or should I say, was constrained to allow him to go.

The three-mile trip from the airport to the taxi stand where she would catch a ride was a nightmare. The distracted mother cried, screamed and accused me of making her do what she should not have done. She became hysterical.

I returned to school and found one of her class friends, prayed with them and, even though the rain continued to pour down, I took them into town for a taxi to Nyankunde. Fortunately, her husband agreed that I had done the right thing for their child. By now it was almost midday. All afternoon I waited for a call from the hospital either with good news or otherwise, but nothing came. Eventually I was called by the friends at Nyankunde around seven o'clock in the evening and was told that the mother had just arrived. The taxi had become stuck on the mud road and took more than six hours to arrive. When they arrived at the hospital the child was sitting up in bed laughing. His life had been spared and the mother was comforted to see him. The little boy continued to have crisis attacks during his parents' time at the Bible School, but I am glad to say none as stressful as this episode.

Although it was a Bible School yet, for teachers and students alike, it was a training school of experience where we learned how God provides at the right time and in the right place. It was also a training school in prayer and how God answers prayer when we are totally cast on Him. Bunia Theological College was a training school in trust as we waited for Him to work out His purposes in our lives. Even though I was the teacher, God taught me many lessons.

I will never forget early one Monday morning as I prepared for classes later that day, a radio message came through from the MAF pilots in Nairobi. The message simply said that my Dad had passed away suddenly the day before. I knew that my Dad had been failing in health, but this news came as a complete shock. My Mother had faithfully written to me each week since I left home for Congo and so I still felt I was very much part of our family unit. By correspondence I kept involved in all that was going on. On receiving the sad news of Daddy's death I felt so alone. I knew all the family would be together at our home in Broughshane while I was thousands of miles away with no possibility of getting home in time for the funeral.

People started to arrive at my home within a few minutes. They were coming to sympathise with me even though my African friends did not know my father. They were well qualified to empathise with me for most of them had already been touched by grief and lost family members, and therefore knew how I was feeling and how to comfort me. All day that Monday my home was crowded with students, church people, Greek and Indian business people and fellow missionaries. Arrangements were made for me to fly home the next day, but the connecting flights did not allow me to arrive before the funeral.

On Tuesday morning before I left Bunia, two of the students came to speak to me privately. They gave me an envelope, which contained a page on which they had written, "We know that Ireland is a long way from Bunia and that you will need a cup of tea on the way. All the students and their wives have given this gift so that you might be able to purchase something to eat for yourself." I was already heartbroken that my Dad had died, but this gesture added a new depth to my emotion. I knew they had barely enough to feed themselves and that they should think of me and give something out of their meagre allowance was so touching and humbling.

Spiritual lessons in God's school are often difficult to learn.

13

Kisangani Here We Come

Long before my time in Zaire, Evangelical Mission groups had made an agreement that each should work and operate in a specific area. When God called me to work with UFM in Zaire in 1976, the region for which the Mission was responsible was Kisangani where, under the leadership of Mr. Jenkinson and at great cost to many dedicated missionary pioneers, dozens of churches had been planted. Sadly, this region that had experienced a tremendous revival twenty years earlier was now off limits to our missionaries because of division in the national leadership of the church.

There were faults on both sides of the different factions in the church and for some years they refused to be reconciled. Consequently the UFM Field Council felt that they could not provide missionary support to either side of a divided church so our missionaries were pulled out of the region. We never ceased to pray that the Lord would bring about a reconciliation of the two factions thus enabling the church and UFM to work together again.

Bunia, to which I had been allocated to teach in the Bible School, was seven hundred kilometres north of the UFM region. Even though our Mission was part of the Joint Mission Board responsible for founding the Bible School, there were no UFM related churches in Bunia or near that region. This meant that my work outside of the Bible School was with the African Inland Churches.

In 1988 God answered the years of prayer for a reconciliation of the churches in the Kisangani region. The Lord had worked in their hearts and there was a very tearful and public reconciliation of the previously discordant camps. God did far above our expectations and after the settlement the Christians' love for each other was stronger than what it had ever been before the damaging rift.

While this reconciliation was happening the Lord independently was urging me to move to the Kisangani area. I loved Bunia and the people with whom I had worked for ten years. During that time I had proved that it had been God's place for me. However, more and more, thoughts of the Kisangani area and a constraint to move there kept coming before me. I was due to travel to Northern Ireland for another furlough, but deep in my heart I knew I probably would not return to live and work in Bunia. However, I was not sure where I would go. The churches in Kisangani were not yet ready to receive missionaries again, but furlough would give me a year to mull it over.

During that year I struggled with what the future held. Four months before returning to Zaire the UFM Council in London informed me, "There are no arrangements yet for Kisangani therefore you need to return to the work in Bunia." Although I accepted what they said, I was still not one hundred percent satisfied that this was God's way for me. I focused my prayers on asking God to make His way clear.

The next evening, after a missionary meeting in Belfast, I called with Edward and Hilde Morrow who were also UFM missionaries in Zaire. They had worked in Kisangani prior to 1978 and were aware of the situation there. Over a cup of tea we chatted about various issues of mutual interest. In time we touched on the current situation in Kisangani and where and what I was planning to do when I returned to Zaire.

I shared with them the dilemma I faced and said, "I thought in my heart that God was opening the way for me to go to Kisangani.

Now the Mission Council have told me that not all the authorisation papers have been signed yet, nor have final arrangements been made with the churches there. Until a green light is given by the churches the Mission is advising me to plan on returning to Bunia."

Edward looked at me and smilingly said "We also think God is calling us back to Kisangani." I was shocked, yet excited by what he had said. For the rest of the night we discussed, reasoned, planned and prayed about our return to Kisangani. I think I sang praises and prayed all the way home that night. I went to bed, but there was no sleep. My mind was overactive and my heart overjoyed. I continued to pray and tried to reason and ascertain whether this was God's way or simply our own thoughts and plans. I was afraid of running ahead of God.

The Mission set aside a day for prayer in Belfast. George Rabey, the General Secretary of UFM, was present for the extended prayer time. During that day it was thrilling to hear that Carol Liddiard, who had previously worked in Kisangani, was also contemplating returning to the city. As a result of that prayer day plans were made for Edward to make a trip to survey the possibilities of our returning to the area and for dialogue with the church in Kisangani.

If we were going to Kisangani then there had to be different planning for what I would take back with me at the end of furlough. I knew for sure that I would need a new Land Rover for the ministry there. The weeks and months that followed were extremely busy gathering equipment and making arrangements for the new team bound for Kisangani in the autumn of 1989.

Carol Liddiard had to complete a course of study in Britain late that autumn and this allowed her to leave for Zaire before Christmas. I travelled back to Africa with the Morrows in early autumn, not only happy to be returning, but also with a sense of purpose even though we were not sure how the Lord would work it all out.

On arrival in Zaire we had field meetings with our colleagues in UFM International which is the American Sending Council. They listened to our plans and helped us put together a future strategy for the ministry in Kisangani. Although none of them were planning to move immediately out of their present ministries in North Eastern

Zaire, they were very aware of the situation in Kisangani and very supportive in prayer and counselling with our proposed plans.

Plans changed as Hilde Morrow fell ill and consequently she and Ed had to withdraw from their planned move to Kisangani. Carol and I were devastated with the news of Ed and Hilde's withdrawal. We stopped to ponder, *Should we or should we not proceed with our plans?* Both of us were single and we wondered if the UFM Council would approve our intended move to Kisangani without a man to head up the team. However, after some thought and prayer we were still convinced that God was opening up the way for us to move forward.

The temperature in Kisangani is much higher than in Bunia and the humidity at times is almost unbearable. Added to this, it was almost impossible to have access from Kisangani to a hospital that would have adequate facilities. Any complicated or lengthy medical care would have to be referred to the Mission Hospital in Nyankunde, which was over four hundred and fifty miles away.

I was now back in my old home in Bunia and I knew that the eventual move would be a large upheaval when I started packing up my belongings. Bunia was the 'exit door' for missionaries leaving Zaire and port of entry for those arriving. Families would often drive from their work location to Bunia to finally pack their suitcases before leaving the country. As a result, missionaries would often hand over equipment and household items for which they had no more need and say, "Here, Maizie, I'm sure you could use this".

You can imagine that during those ten years I had accumulated a substantial amount of paraphernalia, more than I could ever use or even had room for. Now I was faced with transporting all this equipment seven hundred kilometres to Kisangani and I didn't know how we were going to do it. There were very few trucks or drivers who would make the trip and even scarcer were those reliable enough to complete the trip.

A German evangelistic team, DIGUNA, with which I worked closely, had trucks, but none that could carry my large container that I had brought from Ireland some years earlier. I refused to go without the container for it would be needed as a secure storage space in Kisangani. In September I consulted with my friends in

DIGUNA and they informed me a truck was coming from Kenya in October and perhaps they could help.

Letters to and from UFM in London, seeking approval and counsel for the way ahead, seemed to get lost in transit and no answer was forthcoming. It was most frustrating. Carol and I waited and waited without a reply. Weeks gave way to months and we were static so we wrote more letters requesting urgent answers. We were also very surprised as we talked with our DIGUNA friends that they too were experiencing difficulties in bringing their large lorry in from Nairobi. It was a timely reminder that we were in Africa and the place of many unexplained delays. I was doing several 'fill-in' jobs both at the church and Bible School in Bunia, but in my heart I wanted to get going to Kisangani.

14

Are We Still Waiting?

I find that waiting is one of the most difficult disciplines of my Christian life. I much prefer to be pushing ahead, but in Africa pushing ahead can be difficult when nobody is in a hurry to push with you. Having already been delayed for nine months by team changes and lost letters, we decided to prepare for the truck we were told to expect in October and bank on permission from London coming through. I should not have been surprised with yet another delay when the truck didn't arrive in October as had been planned. It was then I needed to remind myself that I was back in Africa where delays are part and parcel of every day life.

We spent Christmas in Bunia. We still had not heard if the UFM Council was in agreement with two single ladies moving to Kisangani to start a new team ministry there. Rather than just mark time any longer, Carol and I decided to go to Kisangani in January. We wanted to survey the situation for ourselves. If permission was granted we would need to find somewhere to live and also discover how we could best serve the Lord in that area.

We set off for a visit to Kisangani early in January and the situation in this new area nearly blew our minds. The houses that had been recommended would need total renovation. Window frames were rotting, toilets did not function, the kitchens were dilapidated, ceilings were down and the floors were up. Just about everything needed attention. After surveying various possibilities and long discussions with the church leaders, it was decided that Carol would work with the women while I would teach in the Bible School at Banjwade. I was also appointed to become the church treasurer!

The churches in Kisangani wanted us to move as quickly as possible, but there was still no authorisation from UFM in Britain for us. We understood the dilemma the UFM Council faced and knew it would not be easy for them to consent to send two single ladies into a formidable situation.

When we returned to Bunia we decided that even if the letter did not arrive from UFM we would plan to move. That same afternoon we happened to meet the team leader from DIGUNA on the road. He told us his group was also keen for us to move to Kisangani so we could work with them from the town. Their ministry was to many millions of people all across Africa and much of the literature they used was from the Every Home Crusade in Belfast. As yet, they had no base in Kisangani and were keen for us to help them break into this new area.

As we chatted he told me that their large truck had arrived from Kenya the previous day. This was the one they had been expecting in October, but it finally arrived in January. Three months delay is not too bad when you are in a hurry in Zaire. Now that the truck and crew had arrived in Bunia we wanted to know if they would be able to transport our belongings, and when. That brought another frustrating reply, "We have a team ministry and I cannot make that decision. You will need to come to Bogoro and meet the team. Why don't you drive out this evening?"

We had travelled twenty-five kilometres of that rocky road to Bogoro many times in Shirley's little Beetle. It was always a bone-shaking ride and took its toll on a small car, but now that my Land Rover had arrived we could negotiate the rough ride a lot better. Even though we had just come back from Kisangani that afternoon it didn't seem to matter how tired we were. Carol and I were very anxious to talk things over with this team and see if we could make any headway, but we were not to receive the sort of news for which we were hoping.

What became evident that night was that the party who came with the truck wished to return to Kenya after one week. We still wanted to know if that would give them enough time to help us. However, a little matter from the past arose that would ease matters. The truck driver happened to be a fellow, who during a previous visit to Zaire, spent many months in my home in Bunia. It was like his second home. I always remember he had a liking for the fresh bread our good cook baked. He regularly helped himself to a feast of bread and butter in my kitchen when on his way through Bunia. When the question of us moving to Kisangani was put to him his answer was music to our ears, "Of course we will move Maizie and Carol to Kisangani, but they will need to have everything packed ready by 6 a.m. on Monday morning."

This was Thursday night. Have you ever packed a house with ten years 'living' in two days? We really didn't have to pack it as such, but we did have to have everything ready to put into the container. First the empty container had to be loaded by a winch on to the truck and then we could load our belongings. The Lord helped us and everything went like clockwork. By Monday afternoon everything was loaded into the container and the men and truck were able to leave that same day. One driver drove my Land Rover the 700 kilometres to Kisangani and Carol went with him. I stayed behind to see the container leave Bunia and then flew to Kisangani the next day. I arrived there only a few hours ahead of Carol and in a short time we were ready for the new work to which God had called us.

The container arrived intact, but Martin, the DIGUNA team leader, didn't. He is six and a half feet tall and the bad roads had caused him to 'knock his back out' so he spent the next couple of days flat on the floor trying to rest and recuperate. He didn't get much of an opportunity as the Christians in Kisangani were so glad to see us they flocked to the house where we were staying. Our arrival was another proof that God had reconciled the previously divided factions and encouraged them to work together with us to see the Lord build His Church in the Kisangani region. There seemed to be no end of the gifts of fruit and vegetables which the Christians brought to our house daily. Even though they had much less of this world's goods than the missionaries, yet they wanted to show their love toward us.

Kisangani was a new town for us with new laws, new policemen to get to know, new shopkeepers who would need to trust us - financial dealings in Congo often demand trust. During the first week I parked in an unmarked illegal parking space. Because there were no signs and I was new to the town I was not aware I was committing an infringement of a traffic law, but everyone else seemed to be aware of it. The policeman who accosted me was quite sharp to begin with, but when I replied in Swahili and told him that Bunia police would not do that, he was very apologetic and told me, "Don't park there again". I never did.

After the members of the DIGUNA team unloaded the container and our baggage they were on their way back to Bunia well laden with thousands of litres of diesel for future evangelistic trips. Diesel prices in Kisangani were a lot cheaper than in Bunia so the trip was a well worthwhile venture for them.

Our next days were spent greeting the hundreds of people who came to visit us. We wondered how we would ever get to know who was who. We listened with interest to what God was doing in different little congregations and we found it thrilling that God had called us to work alongside these people. We planned to be initially involved in training workers to support the expansion of the church. Of course, everyone who came to the house wanted to help us. Often we would say "We need to wait and see what our work will involve before we promise anything."

After a few weeks in Kisangani our first letters to the new postal address arrived and among them was a letter from UFM London informing us that they had approved our plan to move to Kisangani. This confirmed God's guidance to us.

Repairing the dilapidated houses was frustrating, but brought a lot of amusement when we looked back over the events of each day.

There was a large unused front entrance to the two houses which, for security reasons, needed to be blocked off. An 'expert' brick-layer was recommended to us to join the two walls on either side of the entrance. It seemed to be a fairly simple job. However, he laid the bricks on top of the tiled floor because there was a security gate on the outside. I left him with the cement and bricks and went my way.

I returned one hour later only to discover he had built a wall on one side of the entrance up to about a metre high, but he had not followed the line of the tiles. The wall was no more straight than a dog's hind leg. Not being noted for being behind the door, I pointed out that the wall was off line, but he could not or would not see that it was not straight. His reply was. "Don't worry mama, it will meet at the other side." The walls eventually did meet, but that curved wall still stands intact to this day.

Another saga was when we wanted to build up a damaged wall which supported the large gates into our yard. I think the bricklayer found it difficult to accept that I, a white woman, should know how to build a wall. He tried to convince me that he could build a free-standing wall on which we could hang our heavy yard gates. He tried to assure me they would hang for years. I recalled that his last attempt had only lasted four months and that was why they were broken down. When I arrived home from town with the reinforcing rods, he realised I was serious. Thereafter, I checked on him every half-hour to make sure he was following the plan, but even then he tried to take short cuts. I had to insist he did it properly. Eventually he completed the wall and amazingly, it still stands unbroken.

These anecdotes are only about the builder. I could write a whole book about the plumber, the carpenter, the painter, and each volume would be a marathon. We asked an American who had lived in town for ten years or more to recommend a good plumber to us. His reply was, "If you find one would you pass his name on to me?"

He too had many frustrating experiences with local workmen and none of them were satisfactory. I think we had about ten carpenters before we found one that could do a half-decent job without stealing the nails, hammer and other items they could get their hands on. One of our plumbers assured us that he knew what he was doing. Experience had taught me to keep a tight eye on their work even though this meant I got little else done. This particular plumber was laying a pipe to bring mains water into our house. The existing pipe was very rusted and leaking with the result that a lot of water was being wasted. When he looked at the rusted pipe he picked up the new one I had supplied and told me he was going down the road to cut the pipe on some machine.

I asked him if he had measured the existing pipe and offered him a tape measure. He assured me he never used one and he had been at his job for so many years and knew what he was doing. Could I not trust him?   I tried to convince the man that although I trusted his judgement he really should measure the pipe properly. He bluntly disagreed with me and off he went to cut the four-metre pipe. I measured the old pipe in his absence and noted he would need a pipe 2.75 metres long. Sure enough, when he arrived back he discovered he had cut the pipe too short, it was 2.50 metres! The normal way to join a pipe in Zaire is with bicycle tubing and he was all set to do a Zairian joint and leave it a metre underground. My Ballymena upbringing made me frustrated when we had to buy another new length of pipe. I knew we had a lot of other plumbing jobs so the short pipes would be used in other parts of the house, but there was no way that plumber was invited to do any more work for us.

The toilet in my house was also a disaster. When the house had been built the sewerage pipes had been installed under the bedroom, the living room and veranda before reaching the outside down pipe. Of course, it was not functioning when we arrived and according to what we had been told the sewer pipe had been blocked for approximately five years. To unblock the toilet all these floors had to be lifted and I inquired who we might get to do that job.

One day as I turned in at our gate a man waved at me as though he knew me. Later that afternoon the same man came to visit me. When he introduced himself I recognised him. He was the ex-governor of the region and I had met him a couple of times in Bunia. He had come to welcome us to Kisangani and invited Carol and me to his home for a Coca-Cola. In the course of the conversation he asked if he could help with anything. We needed help with a lot of things and took the opportunity to ask if he knew of any plumbers. He said he knew the best plumber in Kisangani.

In a few days that plumber came to see us and he was as good as the former governor had said. The same plumber became our good friend and helped us many a time since, however the toilet saga took a long time to solve. After we installed a new toilet we discovered that the toilet bowl was lower than the end of the sewerage pipes. You've guessed it! Sewerage does not run uphill. In the end we had to build a new septic tank outside, but this time we built it near to the toilet.

All this practical work was time consuming and costly, yet at the same time, it gave us many contacts. We soon got to know many Kisangani people in a short time. We also found that shopping for materials, spare parts, new parts and second-hand parts brought us into contact with a wide circle of the local community. These contacts led to lasting friendships, which in turn would develop into open doors and give us opportunities to share with them the real reason why we had arrived in Kisangani.

Photographic
Section

Open Air Bible
Club - sifu sifu

Sunday School at Sukisa.

Calling the Children to Bible Club

Bunia seminary wives and their ministry to children.

Happy to be graduating after 3 year's of study at the Bunia
Seminary.

Driving on Congo roads always presents a challenge!!!

The River plays an important role in the life of the people of Kisangani whether through its provision of fish or a means of transport to the many riverside markets.

Teaching Pastor's wives at Banjwade Bible School in preparation for their future ministry. Many of these wives will return to lead women's ministry and literacy classes in their villages.

Travelling to a village seminar by bicycle, tiredness is soon forgotten by the eagerness of the students wanting to learn His Word. Inside at work and outside the classroom relaxing.

In Congo a woman's work is never done - from working in the garden to preparing food.

(Below) Willing cooks at a Pastor's Conference.

Gifts of Bicycles at Pastor's Conference

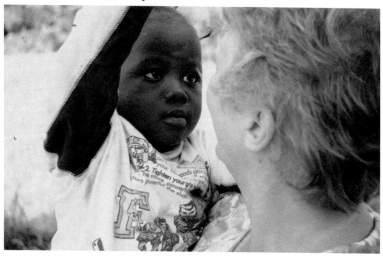

Yet another child called Maizie!

Fishing with baskets at Stanley Falls, Kisangani

The Kisangani
young people
gathered for their
end of year seminar.

Hazardous trips to Village Bible Schools are soon forgotten as we share in the happy ceremony of graduation. (as below)

Young people play an important part in the Congolese church today

Rev. Massini one of the first converts through the work of UFM missionaries together with Bishop Mehuma the present president of the CNCA churches.

June 2002 Maizie shares with Linenga and Katembo who were finalists at Bunia Theological School. Both are now in full time Christian ministry.

Nyankunde Hospital General Assembly meeting June 2002. These are representatives from seven participating churches together with heads of departments. Some of these men lost their lives in the September 2002 massacres.

15

Am I in God's Place?

Settling into a new work in Africa always takes time. Kisangani is the capital of the Upper Zaire region and that meant that there were many official functions to attend. The headquarters of the umbrella group of evangelical Protestant churches was there and the leaders from the various churches would frequently come together for meetings. Many of these leaders were former students from Bunia and it was always a joy to renew fellowship with them. Many of them had 'been trained at Maizie's kitchen sink'. When possible they would stay in my home.

The opportunities for ministry in Kisangani and surrounding areas were so great that at times I felt overwhelmed by it all. More and more I was convinced that the only way ahead was to train the young people to do the work of the ministry. I encouraged the youth to go for good education both at secondary and university level. This was difficult for many because of a lack of funds to cover their fees. Seeing I had encouraged them I felt somewhat responsible so ended up offering employment to them for work around the yard. In this way they were not receiving handouts of easy money and were able to earn enough to keep them at school.

Because our church in Kisangani had been a founder member of the Bunia Theological Seminary Board it meant that three delegates from the church had to participate in their annual council meetings. I was chosen to be one of the three and had to travel to Bunia for the Board meeting. This gave me an opportunity to renew fellowship with so many friends that I had grown to love during the eleven years I had worked there.

Carol continued in her women's work, but was feeling so unwell she decided to accompany me on the trip and have medical tests at the Nyankunde hospital. Furthermore, we had been in Kisangani for almost six months and it was a welcome break to leave the intense humidity of the region for the cooler climes of Bunia. At Nyankunde hospital Carol was diagnosed to be in need of major surgery and had to make an immediate decision to travel home to the UK the following day. I was devastated. We had waited so long to actually get in to Kisangani and then several months to fix up our accommodation. Now, just when everything was taking shape, Carol had to leave.

Early the next morning I was at Bunia airport to see Carol on her way. As I waved goodbye when the aircraft taxied down the runway I was thinking, *What does the future now hold?* I knew that UFM would not be keen for me to live in Kisangani alone. Those were the pre-electronic-mail days and the old fashioned snail-mail to London took at least three weeks to arrive. I could have returned to Kisangani later that same day and waited for the rest to unfold. Instead I went back to the guesthouse in Bunia and had breakfast. Later, in my room, I picked up Daily Light and read the portion for that day, July 12:

> "My Presence shall go with thee, and I will give thee rest. Be strong and of a good courage, fear not, nor be afraid of them: for the Lord thy God, He it is that doth go with thee; He will not fail thee, nor forsake thee: fear not, neither be dismayed. - Have not I commanded thee? Be strong and of a good courage; be not afraid, neither be thou dismayed: for the Lord thy God is with thee whithersoever thou goest. - In all thy ways acknowledge Him, and he shall direct thy paths."

Back in Kisangani I was thankful that the church assigned me to help in the young people's department. This gave me great opportunity to meet with many different groups in the region. One of the first trips I made was to Banalia, which is 128 kilometres from Kisangani. It was in Banalia that many missionaries had been martyred in the Simba uprising of 1964. Among those who were martyred for the Saviour in this place was UFM missionary Ruby Gray, another single girl from Northern Ireland. Ruby had paid the ultimate price of martyrdom for taking God's Word 'into all the world'.

A special weekend had been arranged for the senior pastors who had been appointed to leadership positions and had never been married in church. Some of these couples had been together for over thirty years and had been legally married, but never received a blessing on their vows in a church wedding. They were now putting that right and afterwards there was great celebration. A large crowd of people had come and many activities had been arranged. The highlight for me was a choir of fifty young people who had walked three hundred and fifty miles on a round trip from Lulabunga just to sing at their pastor's wedding. They had not been invited, but had decided they were not going to miss it.

In Lulabunga the young people heard that missionaries had arrived in their area, but they had not yet met them. When I arrived at Banalia it seemed as if their weekend was complete. They decided to take advantage of my visit and planned to have a seminar on Saturday and then a youth rally that night. I spent Friday night putting together a seminar for the next day. The only problem was that the seminar would have to be given in Lingala and I was still in the early stages of learning it. My Lingala teacher was there for the wedding and said, "Do not fear. This is a great opportunity for these young people, so don't miss it. You write out what you want to say and I will correct your Lingala and then you can use that."

The hurricane lamp burned late that night as I struggled through the lessons. On Saturday morning the teacher corrected my paper and by 10 a.m. the seminar had started. We had a great day until we came to the evening rally. I had thoroughly enjoyed the day, but when it came time for me to speak darkness had fallen and we had to use oil lamps. The soft glow from the hurricane lamps, which hung from the cross beams of the church, only illuminated the place sufficiently to see where you were going and recognise people. There was no way I could read my prepared Lingala notes even if they had been in large print.

Urgent prayers went up to heaven and thankfully immediate answers were given. The Lord took over and the lesson came freely to me in Lingala so that I was able to say what I wanted to say. Afterwards, many of the young people asked us to pray with them as they called upon God for forgiveness and strength to live the Christian life. Many of these had trusted the Lord as children, but had little or no understanding of what it meant to walk with God. The seminar was based on the life of Joseph and God had obviously spoken to many hearts through the different practical lessons.

Working alongside senior pastors provided another insight into the Congolese culture. Swahili had been the main language I had used in Bunia, but now ten years later, I was in Kisangani where one half of the town spoke Swahili and the other half Lingala. The town was literally divided in two, even down to separate church services. We had the choice to either attend a Swahili service or one in Lingala.

It was not so easy when speaking Lingala with individuals. Swahili speakers generally want to learn Lingala as it is the military language of Congo. Lingala is also the language used for many of the Congo pop songs and most people knew them. Only a few Lingala speakers wanted to learn Swahili. To be able to mix amongst both communities I had to learn both languages. I found it amusing that I was now speaking four languages and yet I could not forget the day my schoolteacher in Ballymena refused to let me take an English exam because I would be wasting the government's money. I have proved that when God calls He also equips and only the Lord could do this miracle for me.

Pastor Masini (he gained this name because on the day he was born the first machine/bicycle arrived in his village) was designated as my teacher. He was already in his seventies, but he knew how to teach for he had been a schoolteacher all his working life. Every morning I had a one-hour lesson with him and rarely opened the lesson book again until around nine o'clock in the evening when I sat down to struggle with the homework. I felt justified in giving little time to study because life was busy and I was out among the people and was hearing Lingala all day and every day. One evening I was exhausted and struggled with the homework. I could hardly understand the exercises and was beyond thinking. Finally, I closed the book and said, "I'll tell him I hadn't time to do the lessons."

Next morning I travelled the three miles to his home and duly told him, "I'm sorry, but I didn't have time to do my homework last night."

He simply looked up at me and said, "No problem; sit down and do it now." There was no way I was getting out of doing those exercises.

For most of his life Pastor Masini had lived in the forest and consequently most of his exercise phrases were stories of wild animals. Some of the animal names I retained, but others passed me by as I thought I would not need to know them. When time for the final exam arrived, a word appeared I had never seen before. He asked, "Please give the meaning of *nsoi*." I reasoned it must be an animal as a lot of animal names begin with 'n'. *What could it be?* I thought. I opted for the forest rat only to discover later that *nsoi* meant 'saliva'. I should have listened more closely to the teacher in the first place.

It was not only during Lingala lessons that I interacted with the senior pastors. Often they would come to my home or I would meet them at meetings in town and travel with them to special services outside Kisangani. The hours spent travelling in the Land Rover were precious. It was then we had time to discuss church issues, family matters and often they related tales of former times. I had never met many of the senior missionaries who had pioneered this work but I came to know them as I listened to these pastors talk so warmly of their missionary colleagues.

Pastor Bo Martin was one of the outstanding veteran pastors. His identical twin brother was Bishop Assani who at that time was President of the UFM related Church group. Both of these men were outstanding heroes of the faith and, at personal cost and risk to their own lives, had sacrificed much to protect the missionaries during the notorious Simba uprising. Pastor Bo had been an evangelist for decades and there were few places in the Upper Zaire region that he had not covered either by bicycle or motorcycle. His love for the Word of God and His knowledge of it was something special. In 1990 he was diagnosed with throat cancer and was therefore unable to carry on his ministry. The debilitating illness left him really weak and often confined to bed, but that did not deter him from either reading the Scriptures or sharing the gospel. When I went to Kisangani he was living at his home almost eight kilometres from the centre of Kisangani. As often as possible I would travel out to see him and he was not only glad to see visitors, but he always had a word from the Bible for them.

Easter Sunday morning is always a special time of celebration in the Congolese church and during that season people often greet each other with "He is risen!" I always rose early on Easter Sunday morning to prepare for church on that special day, but on one such Sunday a great doubt disturbed my mind. Originally four of us had pledged to go to Kisangani as a team, but the Lord had allowed only two of us to arrive there. Now my co-worker, Carol, had to return home and I was left alone. I wondered, *Have I made a big mistake?* There was no one else in the house with whom I could share my doubts. I read God's Word, but had no peace of mind. *What is wrong with me?* I wondered. I had God's promises that His presence would go with me, but I still questioned whether I was really in God's place. I continued to prepare to go to church, but my mind was in turmoil. I even contemplated not going to church that morning, but in Zaire that would be disastrous. People would have noticed that the only white missionary was missing and would come to see why I hadn't gone to church. That would have meant receiving lots of people all day just because I had missed a few hours at church.

I decided I would put a brave face on and go to meet with the Lord's people on the Lord's Day. Perhaps God would have a word for me that Easter Sunday morning. I was just settling down before the service when I received a little note to say that Pastor Bo would like to see me after church. If I decided to travel the eight kilometres to his home others would be aware of the trip because the person who brought the note would soon let others know the content of the letter. The worship service went as usual, but there was nothing to address my doubts and questions.

As I stepped into the Land Rover, at least seven people told me they wanted to ride with me. I had no problem with this, but I soon found out that Pastor Bo did. When we arrived at his home he was lying in his unlit and unpainted bedroom. He had his Bible by his side as he greeted each one, but then said, "Thank you all for coming, but I only sent for Maizie. I have something to say to her. Would the rest of you please leave." With that the group that came with me began to disperse.

"Maizie, did you bring your Bible?" he asked. I assured him I had and soon he was telling me how the Lord had laid me upon his heart that morning and wanted to share with me the Bible passage God had given him. The respected veteran asked me to read from Esther 4: "And who knoweth whether thou art come to the kingdom for such a time as this?"

Bo Martin lifted his head and looked at me in his searching way and said, "I don't know why God wants you to hear this verse, but I know you need it." If he didn't know why he was giving me that word, there was no doubt that I knew the reason. The aged Bo Martin was a man of vision. He went on to speak to me about all the difficulties the church was facing and suggested ways I might be able to help. He elaborated on the unreached Bamboli tribe and who might reach them; the desire of the Bible School students to be taught, but no one qualified to teach them; the endemic tribal problems which are common to so many African countries and which only the gospel can cure; the primary and secondary schools that needed teachers and practical support and the medical clinic that was crying out for help.

He looked at me again and continued, "Often in God's work you will get discouraged and ask questions as to why you are here, but as I read God's Word and prayed this morning, you were much upon my heart. God has given me this word for you."

I was in tears, not so much at what he had said, but because the Lord had answered my doubts and fears through His servant. No one else in Zaire knew my thoughts that day and yet the Lord used this man to answer the misgivings of my heart. I found that it is just like our Lord to meet us in the most unexpected ways.

After the meeting with Bo Martin there was no more question about moving away from Kisangani. I found new joy and contentment in ministering there and waiting for my co-worker and other workers to join me.

Bo Martin remained a constant prayer warrior and counsellor until God took him home in 1992. His funeral spoke volumes of the influence and help he had been to so many people. After a thanksgiving service in the church, people formed a queue of at least one mile long as one by one they came by the open grave, threw a handful of soil into the grave and said what God's servant had meant to them. I stood there for hours. At times I was weeping and other times smiling when I heard one after the other say, "You led me to know Jesus." In life Bo Martin walked in step with his Lord, in the church he was a blessing, encourager and defender of God's people and to the lost this man was an instrument of righteousness in the hand of God.

16

Bible School in Banjwade

Since its small beginnings in 1931 when Rev. H. H. Jenkinson started a church planting programme in Congo's Province Oriental region, the national church in Zaire has known phenomenal growth. The developing church soon became aware of the need for Bible Schools to teach and train their national pastors and evangelists. This training programme followed Paul's advice to Timothy "Be strong in the grace that is in Christ Jesus. And the things you have heard me say in the presence of many witnesses, entrust to reliable men who will also be qualified to teach others." Many of the Zairians wanted to be taught in the Word and help in the growth and witness of the church. UFM committed its workers to do everything necessary to provide that training.

The Seminary at which I had taught in Bunia originally started in Banjwade in 1961 but, due to the political unrest during the Simba Rebellion in 1964 it had to move north to Bunia. Since then UFM missionaries continued to play a large part in the teaching and administration of the Bunia Theological Seminary.

The original school buildings, which were erected in Banjwade for the Bible School, remained intact during the Simba rebellion and were subsequently used for a Bible Institute, which provided a lower level of theological training than Bunia. Admission to Bunia demanded that the candidate should have successfully completed six years' secondary education while at Banjwade we offered courses for those who had three or four years' secondary education. This lower category had many candidates as young people would often start secondary school, but would later have to leave because of economic reasons. Their parents could not afford to let their children remain at school for six years when there was a possibility of them earning much needed money for the family.

Even during the years when the UFM was absent from the region because of the leadership crisis, the Bible School struggled on. Banjwade is a small village located sixty-four kilometres from Kisangani on the road to Buta. I was assigned to teach at the Banjwade Theological Institute and during term time I would drive from Kisangani to Banjwade every Monday morning and stay there until Wednesday lunchtime. My classes were with the pastors' wives and I found the time with them educational, inspiring and at times exhausting. When I went in my Land Rover there was room to take two other trained national pastors to teach two classes in the men's school. This provided good training for the students and spared them the high fees they would have had to pay if the teachers had been full-time.

Living in Kisangani was demanding, but the two nights at Banjwade were a complete contrast. In Banjwade there was no provision for electric lights during the hours of darkness. My accommodation there was in a small mud hut near the centre of the mission village. Evenings were often spent with the teachers sitting around a fire and under the stars discussing various issues. Other evenings were spent with the students, listening to how the Lord was working in their lives. I had met one of the students about three years before he went to the Banjwade Bible School and he shared with me his desire to study and prepare for Christian service. He said there was one stumbling block in his way and, without telling me what it was, he asked me to pray for it. I did pray for him from time to time and was thrilled when he enrolled at the Bible School.

His wife made a great contribution in the classroom. Their twelve-year-old son, their only child, seemed to settle well into the new environment in Banjwade. One evening they invited me to have the evening meal with them. They had so little and yet they wanted me to share in what they had. As we sat around the little cane coffee table in the middle of a bare room the husband told me that his stumbling block had been his wife. She always refused to go to Bible School because she thought that having only one child was degrading. She was sure that if she were only able to produce one son the other students' wives would mock her and therefore she felt very incapable of being a pastor's wife.

The young wife told me they prayed together and read God's Word. Finally, after many days she was convinced that she should step out from her fears and go to Banjwade to study God's Word. It was not an easy decision for her, but over that little table she told of her joy of obeying the Lord and being in class and learning so many new things from the Word. He then leaned across the table and said, "She discovered today that she is with child and her only words to me were, 'Why did I not obey God's call sooner?'"

We had a time of rejoicing in their simple dwelling that night. When she related her testimony to the whole school in early morning devotions there was more joyous emotion. She had proved that when we put God first He has plans for us far above what we could ever imagine. Now she wanted to help others who might be suffering from the same fear and complex.

At the Banjwade weekly classes I mainly taught Old Testament studies, but also gave classes in homiletics and evangelism. This meant I was able to put my training from Ireland and Switzerland to good use. We also followed the pattern I had adopted in Bunia and besides teaching in the classroom we conducted a weekly children's meeting in a nearby village. This meeting attracted children from several other villages nearby including our own student village. I find nothing more enjoyable than sitting in an African village as the sun begins to sink, sharing the good news of the gospel with hundreds of children who are so anxious to hear about the Lord Jesus.

These boys and girls eagerly listened to the Word week after week and it was not surprising when a little girl asked how Jesus could be her Saviour. She was the daughter of one of our students so had heard the gospel many times before. As we showed her the way of salvation from God's Word and how the Lord Jesus died for her, she asked Jesus to come into her heart and cleanse her from sin. Afterward, she thanked the Lord Jesus for dying for her and asked Him to help her confess the name of Jesus. What a joy and thrill to point a little treasure to the Saviour. That night she went home to tell her Mum and Dad the news of her conversion.

Back in my room that night in the small mud hut and by the light of a hurricane lamp, I quickly checked on what I needed to do to be ready for class the next day. A little preparation and I was all set. Just as I finished I was called to say my bath water was ready. An evening bath in Banjwade was with the barest of essentials. It consisted of a bucket of lukewarm water in the middle of a mud hut and beside it, a large flat stone on which to stand. That is a bush bathroom and for me it was a skilled art having a bath without my clothes falling on the wet mud floor, maintaining one's balance on that small flat stone, not to mention trying to wash my hair at the same time.

After a lovely evening meal of monkey meat and rice I settled down beside the fire with some of the teachers in the open yard. Besides being a lovely way to unwind, it also gave the teachers and me time to air ideas about future plans for the school.

At about eight o'clock as we sat around the fire, I saw a woman approaching in the shadows. She went straight to a teacher's wife and spoke to her for a few minutes. The teacher's wife then relayed to me that it was the mother of the little girl who had trusted the Saviour that afternoon. I knew her well for I taught her in Bible School. She came to say her daughter wanted to see me. The teacher's wife had asked if there was anything wrong, but all the mother would say was that her daughter wanted to talk with Miss Maizie.

I picked up my little bamboo torch, which is a piece of bamboo stick filled with elephant grass, coated with palm fat and set alight. I made my way with the mother along the dirt path to the student village. I inquired from the mother what the little girl wanted, but she too was unaware of the purpose of the visit. When we arrived I found the daughter and her older sister sitting separately from the rest of family. Ruta, the older sister, was about thirteen years of age and suffered from sickle cell anaemia. The illness often left her feeling very weak and unable to join other children in their work and play. I sat down between the two sisters and tried to make conversation with them. Ruta spoke up and said she was disturbed because her young sister had said she knew she was going to heaven whereas she had no certainty as to where she was going. I was not sure if the mother knew what was happening so I called her over. In front of her Mum Ruta repeated what she had told me and then added, "How can Jesus live in her heart and He is not in mine?"

One of the most wonderful questions to answer is when a child asks how they can know the Lord. By the light of those torches and in the presence of her mother and sister I read God's Word to Ruta and explained what Jesus Christ had done for us on the cross. After I explained how she could know for sure that she was going to heaven, she spoke up; "I want Jesus to be mine tonight." Under the open canopy of the tropical sky she prayed for forgiveness and with a true sense of need, called on the Lord Jesus to be her Saviour.

It was nearing the end of the school year and Ruta's father was among those graduating. He had been assigned to be an evangelist in a place about three hundred kilometres from Banjwade. Although the graduation day was full of joy yet it was tinged with sadness for we knew that some of us would probably never see each other on earth again.

Several months after the graduation I was invited to speak at a seminar at Aketi, a town four hundred kilometres north of Kisangani. While driving north, as we passed through a roadside village, there we noticed a large crowd of people standing outside one of our UFM churches. We stopped to see what might be happening only to discover that a child from a nearby village had died and this was the funeral. After further enquiry we found out it was little Ruta, the daughter of our evangelist. Apparently she had died very suddenly. It was such a sad day for her family and friends, all of whom were brokenhearted.

We embraced the distraught parents. Their little girl had gone home to be with Jesus and was safe in His tender care. I recalled to the family about the night she had trusted the Lord Jesus in the student village and it was all because her younger sister had gone home and witnessed for her Saviour.

17

River Region

Teaching homiletics in the Bible School provided many opportunities for practical work. Many UFM churches along the banks of the River Congo asked us to conduct young people's seminars for them, but it was very difficult to leave Kisangani because of the commitments at the Bible School. Christmas holidays seemed to be the best time to make such visits so we prayed and asked the Lord to work it all out for us.

Preparations were well advanced and it looked like the trip to the River Congo was going to come off when news came that robbers had broken into a Catholic Mission station down river and some foreigners had been injured. When this news came through, Bishop Assani, President of the UFM related churches, sent word to say that no white woman should travel down river. That put an end to our 'Christmas Seminars'.

The believers in the region of the River Congo did not take easily to Bishop Assani's decision. They sent a delegation to meet him and ask permission for me to travel, assuring him they would take care of me. Permission was granted by the church authorities and soon six teachers and pastoral students left for Mongandzo and Lulabunga.

We knew we could only go so far by canoe so we took our bicycles with us in order to continue our journey over land. For the final year students this was the practical part of their course. We had planned to spend three days in each place and about three and a half weeks for the overall trip. Most of the village people in the region earned their living from the river, which meant a diet of fish everywhere we went. The village paths were lined with banana trees, which provided plenty of bananas for 'lituma' - delicious boiled and pounded bananas, served with the fish.

From the very first night hundreds gathered in each village for the evening sing-a-long followed by a closing Bible message. Before light each morning the local Christians gathered with us for the early morning prayer meeting. Many poured out their hearts to God pleading with Him for their children, that they would come to trust in Him. They cried to God for the sick for He was the only 'doctor' they knew. The nearest health centre was at least one day's journey away and even when they arrived, the nurse might well have gone on a trip and possibly no medicine would be available to treat their illnesses. They found it was much better to have faith in God for He heard their prayers. Simple faith is very often rewarded.

The prayer meeting finished with a cup of sweet tea before beginning the seminar, the theme of which was "What is a Christian and how does one become a Christian? How does a Christian grow?" These aspects of the Christian life were only some of the subjects we taught in the seminars. Each session was supposed to last for ninety minutes, but by the end of the first morning it became evident that we had underestimated our students. They had so many relevant questions that we inevitably needed to spend more time with them. The two-hour break at midday was shortened to thirty minutes and even with this the discussion continued as we munched roasted corn on the cob for the midday meal. Sometimes sugared peanuts and sweet bananas were a welcome change of diet.

For three days the seminars were dominated by more and more profitable questions and great times of fellowship. At nights I collapsed on to the simple bed they had provided for me. When I pulled it out a little from the wall, what had been a four-legged bed, suddenly was reduced to a three-legged one. The fourth leg had been a stack of bricks over which dozens of cockroaches were crawling. I propped the bed up again and in spite of the roaches, lay back for a very good night's sleep.

The routine continued for three days and on the fourth day we rose early to move to the next village farther down river. That was where one of the seminary students fell down the dry toilet, but that is another story. Sometimes after the early morning prayer meeting the older folks would take time to talk about all sorts of subjects. What had been served as hot, sweet tea soon became a cold, sweet drink. Each village provided more and more eager students to study His Word. In one place no one could remember a white person ever staying there overnight so I became the talk of the village. What many of the locals did not know was that I understood their language and so I found it hilarious listening to how they described me - "Her legs are just like ours; look at how small her feet are; look at her hands; doesn't her hair look like the soft grass." One older man, perhaps in his eighties, was very concerned that the sun would burn the top of my head and so ordered one of the locals to bring his straw hat collection that I might choose a new hat. There was one nice hat that fitted me. That was unusual for most of the others fell down over my ears. Although I liked that hat I had to leave the choice to the old man. I kept going back to the one I liked until he finally said, "No, that hat is not for you; the veranda (brim) is far too small." The students and other teachers were in fits of laughter. I never did get a hat.

The outboard motor pushed our dugout canoe along at a steady pace until we finally reached a village on the River Armwimi, a tributary of the Congo. At the top of the steep bank was Mondandzo where we were greeted by hundreds of singing Christians who had gathered to welcome us. Mondandzo was really in the heart of the forest. Even though they had to hunt for their meat they provided us with delicious meals. The diet could have been anything from tortoise, monkey or porcupine to many varieties of fish. Again the students from the surrounding areas came for the seminar and the Lord did a great work. Prior to our arrival there had been quite a lot of division in the whole area, but during the few days we spent there we saw many families reconciled as we taught the Scriptures. Perhaps the greatest breakthrough of all was when the senior pastor recognised he had been at fault in many things and stood up and asked forgiveness of the church.

There were a lot of tears as people got right with each other and with God. Early morning saw people arriving at the pastor's home to ask forgiveness for a wrong attitude they had held for years. They wanted God to cleanse their hearts. That free time between the early morning prayer meeting and the 'sweet tea' was when a lot happened in our part of Africa. At that time the news of the day was discussed; the monkey or porcupine killed for the evening meal; people who had had a disturbed night came to pray and seek counsel. It is most difficult to describe and define that hour yet it is one of the most precious and important hours of the day in village life. Those who had a Bible came to share what they had been reading that morning.

Soon it was time to move from Mongandzo and from there we were to cycle sixty miles to Lula Bunga. Many of the older people in the villages remembered when the Belgians drove vehicles along these roads, but these arteries for transportation were largely overgrown and reduced to narrow pathways where bicycles were the only transport the local population now saw. The people seemed to be particularly concerned that I, a foreign missionary, should have to ride a bicycle through the forest. They considered these paths to be dangerous. Without my knowledge, a few concerned locals decided to consult with the village chief and told him it was a disgrace that he had not provided transport for us. The chief was spurred into action. It just happened that a leading politician came from a nearby village and his soldiers were always in the vicinity in case he returned home. I think the chief spent two days frantically trying to contact the politician to ask permission for two of his soldiers to give transport on their motorcycles for the senior pastor and myself.

Permission was granted and I was shocked when two motorcycles roared into the village and told us to climb aboard. My heart sank. I knew it would be a lot safer on a bicycle than in the hands of these soldiers who at times were a bit reckless, but seeing such an effort had been made there was no way I could refuse.

Off we sped through the forest each of us clinging for all we were worth to the soldiers and followed by the rest of our party on their bicycles. The younger soldier transported the pastor while my driver assured me "I am the experienced driver, but that other fellow is only 'mon petit' - my wee fellow." He was as much as saying, "I have taught him everything he knows."

Speed was not an option on these hazardous roads. When we approached the more dangerous stretches I saw the pastor dismount and walk for several metres before rejoining the motorcyclist again. Each time I asked my driver if I should dismount also to which he answered firmly, "No. Just sit where you are and keep your feet on the footrests. I am an experienced driver. That rider is only 'mon petit.'"

It was obvious that I was a source of amusement for the pastor and for the others who were making almost as much progress on their ordinary bikes as we were making on the motorcycles. At one place, looming up in front of us, was the dirt track which went up a very steep hill. It was littered with many jagged boulders. The pastor dismounted as at other times. Again I inquired if I should do the same and back came the same reply, "No. Just sit where you are and keep your feet on the footrests. I am the experienced driver; he is only 'mon petit'."

He started up the steep incline, but I could tell that he was in third gear and there was no way we would make it to the top. Half way up the hill he tried to change gear with too many revs and the next thing I knew we were skidding up the mountain and then suddenly became stuck. As ordered by the driver, I kept my feet on the footrests, but my sense of humour could be contained no longer when the bike's front wheel went high in the air and down I went with it. The experienced driver stood at the side of his upturned motorcycle with a look of dismay. With a twinkle in my eye I said to him, "My feet are still on the footrests."

I scrambled to my feet and walked to the top of the hill, as I should have done in the first place. When we came to dangerous stretches of the road the pastor decided to dismount and walk, but my driver still refused to let me dismount. Without any warning we hit another slippery patch. His motorcycle went in one direction and we went another, landing in a slippery mud hole. His pride was more hurt than his anatomy and I was a sight for sore eyes.

A bucket of hot water and a lovely meal at Lula Bunga soon made us forget the excitement of the venturesome day. Over three hundred young people had walked for several days to attend this seminar and they were all ready to commence the studies the same evening as we arrived. We had a great time teaching them God's Word and seeing Him at work. For me the most exciting thing was watching some of the students who had graduated from the Bible School the previous year were now taking their place in pastoral work in that region.

One fellow had worked on renovating an old building and it was already functioning as a village Bible School. He rallied others to help him build ten student huts around the school. When I saw it I was very struck by how orderly and clean the village was. I was even more encouraged to find that the pastor's wife was putting into practice her hygiene classes from Bible School. She was also involved in a 'rabbit project' which provided meat for many of the student families. Her evangelism training was useful as she gathered boys and girls in from the surrounding villages and taught them the Word of God. During the time we were there she brought over one hundred children together in the open courtyard so that we could hold a three-day club. I was the first white person many of these children had ever seen so there were endless questions from them in our free time.

The few days in Lula Bunga went by very quickly. The young people drank in God's Word at the seminars and felt they were privileged to receive this teaching in their own villages. The response was lasting, for after I left they formed choirs, organised a Sunday School and youth groups.

Before we left we had to plan our return journey. The two soldiers who had transported us sat through each session and heard God's Word. Just before lunch on the final day we were packing up when a man came running across the compound to the house where we were. "May I speak to the white woman please?" he asked. The pastors did not know him, but showed him a seat and then called me to talk with the stranger. "I have brought a piece of paper," he said, "and I want you to write your full name down on it." I asked the reason for giving my full name. He answered, "My wife is in the maternity clinic and a child is due to be born soon. I wish to call the child by your name."

I spent time chatting with him and explained that my name was for a female and his child might be a boy in which case it would not be suitable. He looked at me as though I had come from outer space and simply said, "It is only you who says that it is a girl's name. Here in this village no one will know the difference and I wish my child to be called by your name." I agreed to his request and gave him my name although I never did hear if there is a boy running around Lula Bunga called Maizie Smyth.

Our motorcycle ride back to Mongandzo only had two spills and we all made it in one piece. There were many stories to relate in Mongandzo as we sat around the fire that evening. The next day was Sunday and we planned to leave after church and head downstream to spend the night in another village. The morning service was packed and the activities stretched well past the normal three hours, but again it was a joy to share fellowship in His Word with so many people. The parting with friends in Mongandzo took a long time because so many wanted to tell us how the Lord was working in their lives.

It was restful to sit back in the canoe in the afternoon sunshine while we made our way down the River Armwimi. Because it was dry season the water level was very low and we had to weave from one side of the river to another to find the deeper channel. A village chief had asked to accompany us on the trip so we had to accommodate him at the last minute.

Black clouds were beginning to roll in, threatening a heavy tropical downpour. Rainy season in Zaire lasts for nine months of the year and believe me, there is nothing worse than being soaked in the middle of the river in a heavy deluge. Not only did the clouds roll in from the east, but they also came from the south. The wind, which generally precedes a coming storm, stirred the muddy river water into a perilous frenzy. Our heavily laden canoe continued to cut its way through the agitated stream with water constantly lapping over the edge of the dugout. While one of our helpers kept scooping the water from the canoe's hull, we prayed with feeling, "Lord please do not let us get soaked today. Please Lord hear us." Although there was still a patch of blue sky above us, we could see the rain on either side. Amazingly not a drop fell on us. The Lord knew what was ahead.

We were going well and had avoided the worst of the storm when suddenly we were jolted to a stop. We had hit a sand bar. That meant the outboard motor had drawn up sand, which ground it to a stop. We had to lift the engine out of the water and have some of the helpers push us off the shallow sand bar to deeper waters. Because of the sand around the propeller, it took a long time to start the engine and be on our way. In fact, we had only been going for a few minutes when the engine faded and died once more.

From where we were stranded, we could see the village to which we were heading in the distance on the other bank of the river, but it was still a long way downstream. Furthermore, darkness was rapidly approaching as the sun sank in the sky. We knew there was no way we could make it in the dark.

However the village chief, who was travelling with us, assured us not to worry as he knew the chief in another village near to where we had stopped and he was sure his friend would accommodate us for the night. When we finally paddled to the edge of the River Armwimi, our passenger chief hurried off to speak to his fellow chief. After ten minutes he returned to tell us the chief said he never accepted visitors after dark so there was no room for us.

Where we had pulled in at the edge of the river, our canoe was alongside another long dugout canoe, which was tied up. We lost no time in making the two canoes our home for the night. The students and pastors were afraid as to how I would make out in these primitive and basic conditions. They were used to sleeping under the stars in the forest, but they were concerned for this missionary. I had a sleeping bag with me and I was soon nestled into it and lying on the flat bottom of our canoe. The rest of our entourage made themselves comfortable in the other one.

Before we retired into our improvised accommodation we thanked the Lord that He had known what was ahead. If it had rained everything would have been soaked and would have made our night even more uncomfortable. As it was, in the absence of lodgings, He had provided us with an extra canoe to make room for everyone to put their head down for a few hours.

Two of the party were appointed to keep watch through the night. I slept for about an hour until the snoring of those who had been appointed to keep watch wakened me. As I lay there the words of Psalm 121 filled my mind,

"He that keepeth thee shall neither slumber...The
Lord is thy keeper; the Lord is thy shade upon
thy right hand. The sun shall not smite thee by day,
nor the moon by night. The Lord
shall preserve thee from all evil...The Lord shall
preserve thy going out and thy coming in from
this time forth, and even for ever-more."

The Psalm taught me that the Lord watches over us and watches out for us. He certainly did that night. The mild air blew gently upon us keeping the rain away, the stars were bright in the sky above and all the forest was filled with its usual nocturnal cacophony of forest and river wildlife. I slept well and as the morning light came up I was ready for the new day.

When I wakened the 'boatman' was already stripping the engine, cleaning it and reassembling each piece in its proper place. He soon got us going again, but he said it was only a temporary job, at least until we crossed the river and landed at our desired destination. On our trip to the other side we jostled with many small canoes which were loaded and piloted by children going to school. The only school for the area was about eight miles down river and each family owned a small family canoe to transport their children. They reminded me of my days back home in Greenhill when I had to ride my bicycle to and from school. Paddling downstream was looked upon as great fun for the children, but it wasn't so enjoyable coming home against the strong current.

The village folk were waiting for us and wondered what had happened on the previous night. They had prepared a hefty breakfast for us, which was another variety of fish. This was followed by a quick wash from a bucket of water and then we were all set to begin our seminar.

While we gave the classes, the boatman had his work cut out for him. He had to make a new piece for the engine to replace the faulty one. On these rivers you can always be sure to find an expert in any field and sure enough there was one in this small village, but he did not have the proper metal for the job. That meant another improvised piece had to be manufactured.

The engine was rebuilt and fixed for the following day when we departed this small village and headed further down river to Basoko. This was more of a town than a village and we knew we could find help there for our ailing engine. At Basoko we were also able to replenish our fuel supply.

With the engine repaired and the fuel drums filled, we were keen to be on our way. However, the Christians at Basoko insisted we stay for one more day and teach a seminar. Instead of leaving early morning as planned, we spent the whole day teaching. In this we again saw God's hand for it rained heavily throughout the day and we could not have travelled on the river in those conditions. News also arrived to say that one of our churches on the opposite bank of the River Congo was waiting for us to spend time with them. They even sent a canoe to Basoko to guide us to their place, which was about sixteen kilometres across stream, not an easy journey when paddling against the swift-flowing current.

We reached the isolated church late that afternoon and there I saw Christian love demonstrated in a very special way. A sixty-year-old man who had served the Lord faithfully as elder in his congregation which was about forty-eight kilometres into the forest from the river's edge, knew that we had been travelling for some time. That morning he told his wife to make some fresh bread and a pot of stew and then packed the bread, the stew and two flasks of coffee made from his homegrown coffee beans and cycled all the way to the river to wait for us. He was not expecting anything in return for what he had prepared, but simply wanted to express his gratitude that God had brought us to his area. Although we were anxious to be on our way home, we felt compelled to remain there to teach the young people in that area.

By the time we finished this last seminar we had been absent from Kisangani for one month. On the final evening choirs of young people sang as we sat around a fire in the middle of the village. The singing was followed by a message from God's Word. We stayed there until late and although it was long past the hour when we should have been off to bed, we continued by the dying embers of the fire as a young couple told us how they believed God was calling them to Bible School. They were full of questions, "How can we go? Who will support us? Will we be able to study? We have only completed three years at secondary school, will the lessons be too difficult for us?"

It was obvious to us that God had laid a burden on their hearts to teach others for they were already involved in teaching Sunday School and had been part of evangelistic trips into surrounding villages.

For one local man the couple's willingness to go to Bible School was an answer to prayer. He had been praying that God would raise up young people from the villages on the river to reach out to their own people. He was ready to send them to Kisangani with us, but there was no room in our canoe. Furthermore, it was the middle of the academic year so we persuaded him that they would be better waiting until the following year.

Early next morning we boarded the canoe with all those on our entourage. The engine spluttered into life and although it was under par, we slowly made our way up the River Congo. We had to stop periodically to give the engine a clean up before being on our way again. We had planned to spend a night at Isangi, but because of the interruptions, we had to pull in at a village almost fifty kilometres further down river. There was a church where we stopped and the Christians were glad to see us. We received the usual hospitality with choirs turning out to praise God for His goodness. That night the 'boatman', by the light of a hurricane lamp, dismantled the engine yet again to try to get to the bottom of the problem. While he worked on the outboard motor an older man wandered into the gathering and was soon talking with the boatman. "There is your problem. That piece is bent and it can never be repaired," he said, "I may have a piece just like it. I used to be a marine mechanic."

I don't know how long they worked, but by the next morning the engine was sounding healthy again. My part in it all was to hand over the equivalent of £5 to pay for 'the piece'. We roared up the River Congo at a more accelerated pace and after a full day's trip we arrived at the Yakusu hospital where we spent a very comfortable night. We knew we were only twenty-five kilometres from Kisangani so early next morning we arrived home.

In spite of the discomforts, dangers and delays, it had been a month full of blessing. God had done many wonderful things for us. We had not suffered any illness nor did we encounter any great mishaps. Undoubtedly, the most wonderful blessing of all was that many hearts had turned from darkness unto light. However, we did arrive home with a heavy heart because of the challenge of that region. We were full of unanswered questions; *Who would teach these people? Where would we get Bibles for them all?*

I did not have all the answers, but we were more determined to devote our time to training men and women in the Bible School.

18

Ubundu Visit

Since the Simba rebellion of 1964 no missionaries had ever returned to Ubundu. Now at the beginning of 1990 the believers there sent word to say they felt it was time for some one to go and help them. The road to Ubundu was notorious and described as impassable and impossible. However, the Ubundu Christians assured us that they had worked on the road and all was well. Other reports we received confirmed that they had worked hard and the road was greatly improved.

We decided to send a delegation of ten people who had experience in education, medical work, Sunday Schools and youth development. The first one hundred and ten kilometres on the main road went by without incident. When we turned off onto the smaller dirt road leading to Ubundu we noticed that work had indeed been done. It still would not have been considered a class 'A' road, but we reckoned we had only to travel twenty-five kilometres along the track. We knew there was a river to cross, but we met people on the road and they told us the ferry was waiting for us.

When we arrived at the river's edge we discovered the ferry was there, as we had been told, but the 'captain' had gone off to his field, wherever that was. It seemed nothing to the locals that we would have to wait at the market near the ferry for a few hours during the hottest time of the day. Because I was the first white to visit that region for many years I became the centre of attraction. I decided we should not waste our time so we gathered a crowd of children into the shade of a large mango tree where we began to teach them God's Word. We were well removed from the immediate vicinity of the market, which meant we did not need any permission to conduct a meeting in a public place. We need not have been concerned about this for soon the people at the market moved to where we were and this gave us an opportunity to speak to a very large congregation of children and adults. Before long over five hundred people sat under the shade of the various tropical trees at the side of the river and listened to a clear presentation of the Word of God.

Meanwhile, two local Christians had gone to look for the ferry-man. After a couple of hours they returned with the captain and soon we were being transported to the other side of the river. When we arrived there a crowd of believers lined the river bank to welcome us. They were so delighted to see us, that as we drove the Land Rover slowly behind them, they chanted a welcome song for us. Two ladies nearby were discussing about the 'strange white woman'. They had chosen to speak in Swahili and were unaware I could understand all they were saying. I found the comments hilarious to say the least, but I could not remain silent any longer when one of them said, "I wonder what she will eat? Do you think she brought her white food with her?"

I spoke up in Swahili; "I love your cooked bananas and leaves from the cassava plant." If Zairians could blush they would have been the most blushing pair of ladies in Zaire that day.

It was late on Thursday evening when we arrived in Ubundu and sat outside around the fire with the hundreds of people who had walked from the surrounding villages to meet us. Many greetings were exchanged, accompanied by a lot of community singing, and then about nine o'clock we began to teach from God's Word. The choirs sang on well into the night, but we had to reluctantly retire for we were weary from a hard day's travel and were glad to lie down on our grass-filled mattresses.

Friday and Saturday were fully occupied with teaching, discussion, praying and sharing testimonies from early morning to late at night. It was a joy to see many folks putting their lives right with God, others saying "Yes I will obey and do what He is asking me." For me the greatest joy was to see many young people indicating they wanted to go to Bible School. This was an answer to prayer for until that day there was only one trained pastor in the whole area.

Just as the sun was setting on Saturday evening, little groups of people were relaxing on the grass, on deck chairs and on the village paths when suddenly a bird flew overhead making the most weird noise I have ever heard. It sounded like 'Bwa-bwa-bwa.' The cry of that bird brought confusion to the village and sent all the children and young people fleeing toward the forest. Women were calling after the children to take some sort of container with them.

I sat watching all this in amazement until finally someone began to explain. "That bird is called a Bwa-bwa and you often see it walking through the forest."

Once they told me this I recognised the bird, but it looked so different in flight than what it was like on the ground. It had the strangest shaped wings. My informant went on to explain that when those wings are fully-grown, they only last for one flight and the day it flies is the day that a special grub appears on the forest palm trees. The grubs are a speciality not to be missed. That is why the children ran to the forest with containers to collect the rare grubs. When they returned the grubs were cleaned in their traditional way and then cooked for supper. Grubs for supper and grubs for breakfast is not exactly five star treatment in a western home, but I assure you they were delicious.

Sunday started early with crowds flocking to the mission station. The church was filled to overflowing and other people sat under the shade of improvised roofs, made from palm branches which had been tied together. From seven o'clock in the morning until the middle of the afternoon we sang and sang, then listened to God's

Word, sang some more and listened to God's Word again. No one complained that the service was too long. Heaven will even be better than what we experienced in Ubundu, but the joy, the fellowship and sense of God's presence was really like heaven on earth.

Late on Sunday night it started to rain which made us thank the Lord for giving us a rain-free day. However, when the rain started it really did pour down. On Monday morning the humid mist clung to the forest and dampness and mud were all around. Despite the pleas for us to stay for another day we decided we had to return to Kisangani.

The dirt road had been transformed into a quagmire and I knew we would have problems, especially when we came to cross the four bridges made of slippery logs. Arriving at the first log bridge the nine passengers got out of the Land Rover and as I carefully tried to manoeuvre the vehicle across I could feel it slipping and sliding. There were no barrier rails at either side of the bridge so I instinctively gripped firmly to the steering wheel, but that was not enough to stop one side of the Land Rover slipping down between two logs on one side. The drop below was less than a metre, which was reassuring. The Land Rover's transmission was already engaged in four-wheel drive and I knew that would give me enough traction to pull the vehicle out. Steadily and slowly we edged across the bridge until we reached solid ground. A similar breathtaking experience was repeated again at the second bridge and yet again at the third. On each occasion the sturdy Land Rover performed admirably and was able to pull itself out of danger.

When we reached the fourth bridge I was horrified to find that the drop under it was a menacing thirty metres. As I tried to carefully steer the vehicle across the bridge I was dismayed to hear all four wheels drop between the slippery logs. Apparently the previous night's rain had softened the beds which secured the logs on either side of the bridge, consequently there was no way to prevent the logs from separating. With all four wheels sunk between the logs we had to jack up the Land Rover and place a few other logs between those that had parted. Everyone played his or her part to remedy the predicament.

When it came time to position the vital replacement log our hearts sank as we heard a sickening c-r-a-c-k, the log on which the jack rested could not sustain the weight and shattered under the Land Rover. I was heart-broken as I wondered how we would ever get the Land Rover out. All my passengers were experienced cyclists, but not one of them had any experience of coping with this situation of how to pull such a heavy vehicle out of this rut. One of the senior men in our team tried to comfort me by telling me a truck from the local Catholic Mission passed this way every month and it would soon be coming. Then he added, "They passed by Thursday and will be back this way in three weeks and four days."

Discouraged and not knowing what to do, I walked alone into the forest. I must confess that for once, tears flowed. *Lord what will we do? How do we get out of this? Maybe I should have waited another day?*

Two of the older men walked toward me and one said in his simple way, "Let's all get together to pray. Let us pray that God will give us one idea which will be His idea."

After we prayed a young fellow suggested cutting a long log and standing it upright from the bed of the river to support the broken log. To me the idea sounded impractical and bizarre, but I reminded myself that we had asked the Lord for an idea and this was the only one we had come up with. For the next hour the men felled a tree and prepared a log to see if there was any advantage in the young man's suggestion. When the log was placed as a support under the bridge we prayed again. When I climbed into the Land Rover my faith was not too strong that this would work, but I clearly remember grasping the steering wheel and saying, "Lord please take us out of here."

Even though I had prayed I was still a little anxious as I gingerly put the Land Rover into first gear. To my surprise the big Land Rover began to gently pull itself out of the gap and across the bridge to the dirt road. I could never describe the relief and rejoicing I felt in that moment. Within minutes we were back on the last stretch of the dirt track that would take us to the good road leading to Kisangani. However, the emotional trauma and hard work of eleven hours of travel on the twenty-five kilometres of dirt track and tricky bridges had left us exhausted.

The people at the local church on the main road were waiting to welcome us with a meal. They had prepared the food at midday when we were expected but, in spite of cold food with hot gravy, we were soon tucking in.

As we piled back into the Land Rover for the rest of our trip back to Kisangani there was much praise and testimony of God's goodness to us.

19

Provision and Protection

In 1992 Zaire had been politically stable for more than two decades although rumours abounded on every hand. We had been in Kisangani for three years and felt that the time was right to invite Missionary Aviation Fellowship to come to our area to implement their excellent programme of assisting God's servants in isolated areas. I learned that there was to be a conference of MAF pilots in Kinshasa, Zaire's capital, and we decided that we should make representation there. The MAF pilots based at Nyankunde passed through Kisangani on their way to Kinshasa and so I arranged to meet some of them at the Kisangani airport with our papers outlining our request. We had already discussed these plans many times, but the time was now right to make the final move.

Just before lunch on Friday a ten-seater MAF plane flew into Kisangani and for the next hour several experienced pilots discussed the whys and wherefores of our request for a flight programme. On leaving I jokingly remarked to Gary Toews, the Nyankunde pilot, "Watch yourself. You're a country boy going to the big city."

Nyankunde where Gary was based was a small 'bush' station and Kinshasa was the capital of Zaire. He knew that I was due to leave the following day for a trip so his immediate reply was "You take care in the bush." Off they went and I went back home to pack for our journey.

Early next morning we were ready to leave on the six-hundred kilometre trip which would take three days. Pam Bryans, who was planning to move to Kisangani to supervise the national Christian bookshop 'CEDI' was staying in my home and again jokingly over a last cup of tea before we left, I quipped in jest, "If war comes, just leave. Don't worry about the things here or about me."

We planned to spend Sunday at Kole with the local Christians. We had a great Lord's Day and the fellowship was rich. On Monday afternoon we were to continue our journey through a heavily wooded area. Dark clouds began to roll overhead from the north. The wind, which is always the forerunner of heavy rain, increased and rustled through the forest, so we decided to wait until the storm passed over in case some trees might fall on us. As it turned out, this was the Lord's providential care for us. One hour later, when we did venture down this road, we were confronted by twelve fallen trees blocking the way. We would never have been able to get through without tragic consequences.

Several hours were spent clearing the road only to find one hour later that we had to cross the most notorious bridge in our area and this was my first time across it. It was an old railway bridge about one hundred and fifty metres long. Although the bridge had a metal frame, only four boards straddled a very short portion of it. To drive the Land Rover across, it was necessary to edge the vehicle on to the two front boards, then move the back two to the front of the vehicle and repeat this action until we reached the other side. With many frightening moments behind us, we made it safely across one hour later. Finally, at about 8.00 p. m., we arrived exhausted at Aketi.

The hardships of the journey were compensated by a wonderful welcome from the believers, warm water for a lovely 'bath' and then a delicious chicken and peanut-sauce meal. At around ten o'clock I was ready to lie down, but the people would have none of it. Hundreds of young people had walked hundreds of kilometres to be there and they had been waiting most of the day for us to arrive. It was no good trying to explain to them that a storm had delayed our trip. Even though it was late they expected us to teach them the Word of God. Fortunately I had anticipated this might happen and had come well prepared. We taught the Scriptures to this spiritually hungry congregation and no one showed any sign of weariness. Finally, at about one o'clock in the morning, I retired to the grass bed. When I fell asleep the sound of the singing choirs was still echoing into the night air.

On Tuesday morning we got down to the usual business of various seminars with different groups meeting under the separate palm trees and some even enjoyed the comfort of the bamboo benches in the local church. Throughout Tuesday and Wednesday we taught seminars and then on Thursday we had committee meetings. Teaching day after day is physically and mentally draining. Everyone wanted to ask questions and lots of topics were discussed. However the effort was worthwhile and the Lord did a great work in many hearts. It was especially encouraging to teach at the evening sessions and listen to testimonies around the dying embers of a fire.

Everywhere we travelled I usually carried a small radio to listen to BBC World News, but during this trip there had been no spare moments to tune in to the radio. On Thursday morning, as we left the early morning prayer meeting, one of the pastors asked me if I was British. I assured him I was. He then told me that the British Government had issued a statement that morning saying this was the final call for British citizens to leave Zaire immediately.

I was taken aback. The news caused my thoughts to crowd in; *what is happening? Whatever has caused this emergency? What should I do?* There was a real buzz at the breakfast table where we heard that there had been rioting in Kinshasa, Kisangani and many other places. They all looked at me and said, "What will you do?"

I knew there was no way to communicate with my colleagues in Kisangani so I also wondered what I should do. We did what we always did in an emergency, we prayed. The local pastor told me to go the Catholic School and there I would find an elderly Belgian teacher who had a radio with which I would be able to speak to the UFMers in Banalia. Off I went with two national colleagues and soon found the teacher. He had long since celebrated his eightieth birthday and his failing eyesight, deafness and general vagueness did little to reassure me he understood what was happening.

The old man sat down at a table and uncovered a hidden radio. He twisted several wires and started to work at a dial and I wondered who he was going to contact. First he called to someone and asked if there were any messages. The reply was garbled. He lifted the speaker closer to his ear and we could hear very little of what was coming over the air. He spoke in French and kept saying "I can hear you, but I cannot understand you."

I tried to get nearer to the earpiece and soon understood the words "Protestant" and "Smyth." Quickly I said to the elderly teacher "It's a message for me."

The only ear with which he could hear was already tightly pressed to the earpiece so he could not hear me. After calling several times without any success I finally tapped him on the leg and said rather loudly, "That's me."

Finally, he got the message and answered into the microphone, "She is here."

He handed me the apparatus and I sat down to speak to an operator in Buta who told me that the MAF pilots were looking for me. I further learned that Carol Liddiard and the other missionaries from the Baptist and Anglican Mission had already left two days ago and I should get in touch with MAF immediately. The old man's radio did not have the MAF frequency so I could not contact them. It is at such times one wishes they had a list of all the radio frequencies, but even that would have been of no advantage to us for this was a 'fixed frequency' radio.

Using this frequency I was able to contact Norwegian Baptist missionaries at Bondo, which was north of where we were. They were able to make contact with MAF and let them know where I was. They also instructed me, "Drive to Buta and get in touch with us from there."

It was hard to keep up with my thoughts and make decisions while still speaking on the radio. First I wondered how I could leave all my national colleagues stuck here with my vehicle at Aketi. I suggested to the friends on the other end of the line that we arrange another time to talk so as to give me time to discuss the whole matter with the church leaders.

Their committee meeting was in full swing when I took my place among them, but though I tried to listen to the business my thoughts were elsewhere. *How could it all be worked out? How will I get out of here?* While I was mulling over these matters my thoughts were jolted when I was invited to tell the meeting what news I had received from the radio. After I told the assembled elders the predicament, much discussion took place. The leaders were more decisive than I was and said I must drive the one hundred and sixty kilometres to Buta the next day. I was saddened by this interruption to our plans, but willingly agreed to do what they had determined.

Many of these men had been through rebellion before and knew that these things did not blow over in a day. Rev. Tchakua, one of the men present, had secretly supplied food for Mr. & Mrs. Jenkinson, our senior missionaries, during the tragic troubles in the 1960s.

After the whole congregation prayed for the situation and me, Rev. Tchakua came right from the back of the church to where I stood at the front and took my hand. He spoke up so all the assembled group could hear what he had to say, "God brought you here, God will take you home and God will bring you back again." He then quoted Psalm 121 "The Lord shall preserve thy going out and thy coming in from this time forth, and even for ever more."

I returned to the radio and told the Norwegian friends I would drive to Buta on Friday as they had suggested. Thursday night was memorable as we shared from God's Word around the fire. We prayed much for the families of our colleagues in war-torn Kisangani. We also wondered about and prayed for the families of the national pastors who were with me. Other questions arose around the fire, "How had the missionaries got out of Kisangani? What about the pilots who had gone to Kinshasa for their conference? Did they make it home or were they trapped there? What about the mission property?" On and on the questions arose and on and on we prayed. After the prayer time it was decided that two of the church leaders should travel with me to Buta to look for a driver who would be able to take the Land Rover back to Banalia.

Early the next morning we were on our way. We had to cross the treacherous bridge again where we repeated the same tedious operation of rotationally placing planks of wood in front of the vehicle's wheels. Arriving in Buta we found there were soldiers at every corner. I called the MAF from the mission and was told that if there were soldiers in Buta they would not come. That meant I would have to drive another hundred kilometres north to Malingiwa.

After eating some roasted corn to keep hunger at bay, we were on our way. It was not difficult to sense that people were very afraid. However, no one mentioned that there were serious political problems around. We made good progress, but darkness began to fall about six o'clock. We felt we should be near Malingiwa. Pastor Safiko, one of our elderly leaders, who accompanied me, said that he was sure we would not find any food in Malingiwa as the people would have already eaten what supplies of food they might have had.   Even as he spoke it struck us how hungry we were. The roasted corn from midday was long finished and we did not have another crumb between us.

There was not a house in sight and the forest was dense on either side of the road. If there was no food in Malingiwa I wondered what we were going to do? Less than two minutes after Pastor Safiko commented about the lack of food in Malingiwa, a man stepped out of the thick forest with a live antelope over his shoulder. He frantically gesticulated at us to stop, which we willingly did. Soon the stranger was pouring out a story about his sick child in his isolated home in the forest. He added that he had no money to buy medicines and if we would only buy this antelope it would help save his child. Not only was God's timing perfect, but His provision was also abundant. I had enough money with me and was able to make the purchase. We had helped the poor man, had plenty of food for us and enough to provide a meal for the church leaders at Malingiwa. Barbecued antelope never tasted better than the feast we shared with our friends for supper that night.

After supper, some beds were found, hot water was provided and we closed the day with a prayer-time around the customary fire. One item of news I heard at the fireside really amazed me. A local pastor told us of how their two-way radio had not been working for nearly a year. They were deep in the forest and had had no contact with the other church or hospital groups. Just the previous weekend a French tourist stopped with them for a night and as they chatted he told them he was a radio technician. The pastor decided to take advantage of the stranger being there, so out came the two-way radio, and after the man fiddled at the radio's innards for a short time, it crackled into life. We recognised another token of the Lord's care for us in sending the French technician to that remote area just at the right time. He knew we would need that radio in this emergency. Our prayers were mingled with praise as we concluded our time together before retiring to bed.

Next morning we strung the antenna up on a large orange tree and at the same time took advantage of picking some oranges which gave us fresh orange juice for breakfast. Once the pastor's radio had been set up I was able to call MAF. My pilot friend Gary Toews answered the call and could not believe that I was in Malingiwa and that the radio was working. Within three hours a pilot was on his way in MAF's Cessna aircraft to pick up two missionaries in Bondo and me in Malingiwa. When I stood with my dear friends, the senior leaders, on Malingiwa's airstrip we all cried. Some of the men were in their seventies and anxious about their families back in Kisangani. I felt guilty having to leave them. What did the future hold for them? We had seen so much of God's hand providing and protecting us that it gave us confidence to trust Him at this troubled time. The Lord had brought us safely to Aketi and on to Malingiwa. Now that we were going our separate ways I knew He would watch over us as we parted and hopefully bring us back together again.

Before embarking on the small aircraft, we agreed that I should plan to stay in Britain for three months. The plane taxied down the runway and up into the air. I kept waving at our friends below and they all responded by waving their arms in the air. The plane banked to the right and the leaders were out of sight, but my heart was heavy for my colleagues, yet rejoicing in how God had led us all the way.

When I boarded the MAF plane I was still wearing my African clothes as I had no other clothing with me. I had left Kisangani planning to spend two weeks in the bush before returning there again. The emergency changed all of those plans, but there was no possibility of retrieving my wardrobe. Fellow UFM missionary from Belfast, Anne Magowan, came to the rescue and kindly provided me with more appropriate clothing to go to London so I travelled home 'in style'.

Later I learned that my national co-workers had returned to Kisangani four days later and were glad to find that God had protected their families just as He had shielded us. Truly we serve a great God who is always faithful.

20

Sleeping Through the Storm

I was able to return to Zaire within the three months I had planned, but political tensions continued to increase. To try and solve the unstable and potentially dangerous situation, President Mobutu decided to call a National conference in Kinshasa and our church leader, Bishop Assani, was invited to attend. The purpose of the conference was to give representatives from every area of Zairian life the opportunity to be present. It had been planned that the convocation would last for one month, but it became very drawn out and far exceeded the original time allotted. Rumours and counter rumours ran rife about the political future of the country.

After the national conference had been going for about three months, someone came running to our home one Sunday morning to say that the Bishop had died in Kinshasa, the capital. Kinshasa was hundreds of kilometres away from Kisangani and there was no telephone communication between the two places. Consequently, there was no way of knowing if the news of the Bishop's death was a rumour or was really true. To make matters worse, because it was

Sunday no private two-way radios would be operational. We felt helpless and did not know what we could do.

Some of us went to church that Sunday morning, but as the rumour spread through town everyone made their way to the Bishop's residence for the 'wake'. My house shared the same yard and was next door to the Bishop's home. In fact, with so many people sitting around, I knew I needed to make tea. They had come for a wake, but there was no body and everyone wanted to know if the news was really true. The Bishop's wife was at home and she was not convinced that it was so.

Suddenly there was a loud racket outside and with it another surge of people pressed into the yard swelling the crowd already there. I went out to see who it was, only to meet members of the Bishop's close family arriving from Banalia, which was one hundred and twenty-eight kilometres away. I concluded that the news had already reached Banalia, which was the Bishop's home territory. They told us of many other people they passed on the road making their way to the Bishop's wake. Seemingly, the boatmen on the ferry at Banalia refused to cross the River Arumwimi as they were waiting to transport the Bishop's body across. I thought this must have been more than a rumour if it had gone this far.

Meanwhile, I had to get busy in the kitchen for these new arrivals needed to be fed and crowds of other visitors would spend the night sitting in our yard. Even while I worked in the kitchen and people were coming and going, I kept turning over in my mind how I could find out what the truth was about my friend and neighbour, Bishop Assani.

Early on Monday morning I was on the radio trying to make contact with Kinshasa. When I got through to someone, they also had heard the news, but thought it was a rumour. It seemed impossible to track down anyone in that large city who was able to confirm the truth. I asked my contact to try to have Bishop Assani speak to me on the radio so we could put an end to the tittle-tattle. The contact said it was not possible to reach the Bishop as he would be in conference.

Several of us had been asking the Lord to please help find out the truth, but every time we tried we drew a blank. If we had confirmation that he was alive then the hundreds of people who were sitting around our yard could go home, but while there was no news to the contrary the mass of people refused to go home. Without speaking to the Bishop himself no one would believe us that he was still alive. His poor family was very distraught with the uncertainty, but his wife maintained her husband was still alive.

Bright ideas do not come to me very often, but suddenly I had a brain-wave. I knew the conference was televised each day and if the television cameras focused on the bishop in the meetings that would dispel all rumours. It was most improbable that it should happen, but it was worth a try. A few of us went to the local radio station where one of our Christians worked and asked for his help. He knew all about the rumour and was as concerned as other people in town, but when I explained my bright idea to him he decided to give his assistance.

We sat waiting at the television screens and in less than two hours, we all saw our friend Bishop Assani listening attentively to the debate in the conference. If anybody had missed seeing him the first time there were plenty of other opportunities for it seemed that every half hour we caught another glimpse of him sitting in his designated place. This was another answer to prayer and allowed many people to return home satisfied that their great friend was still alive.

The weeks passed and although Bishop Assani had not returned home, we took it for granted that all was well. The conference was on the news every day and everyone knew it had become a very drawn out affair.

One quiet Sunday evening I sat outside the house talking with my neighbours and enjoying the coolness which descended after dark. On Sundays most Zairians go to bed early and that night was no exception. By nine o'clock I was lying on top of my bed under the protection of the mosquito net. I was reading a book, which had been an early Christmas present. I was enjoying the book so much that by midnight I still had not slept, but decided it was time to close my eyes and try to sleep.

It seemed I was not long over to sleep when suddenly, loud banging awakened me. I was startled by the reverberating noise and speculated what it could be. Just then a roar of distant gunfire broke the stillness of the night and echoed around the house. While living alone I had become accustomed to speaking to myself so I asked audibly, *What on earth is happening? Is this a dream?*

I could hear the night guards speaking to each other in loud whispers so I opened the window and asked if they had heard the racket. They assured me it was definitely gunfire from the other side of the River Congo. The thick darkness of the night seemed impenetrable and we stared into nothingness knowing that dawn was soon to break. Many questions and suggestions about what it might be were exchanged between the guards and myself. However, we did not have to wait long to find out the reason for the disruption.

As dawn broke we could see truck loads of soldiers making their way across the river towards our side of town. It was a terrifying scene when they started shooting up and down the road and from every corner. It did not take long to discover that this was no picnic. The soldiers were in revolt because the government had introduced new bank notes and rumour had it that the soldiers were to be paid with them that day. Apparently no one wanted the new currency, including the soldiers, and this was their way of showing opposition to the government's economic policy.

No one dared leave their homes, but watched from behind the closed doors and in the shade of their curtains as the soldiers imposed their rule on the town. By lunchtime we knew that several stores had been pillaged and looted. From my house we could see the looted merchandise being transported to various homes.

God's Word is always precious in perilous times and a scripture text sent to me by some friends proved to be a real source of comfort; Isaiah 41:10 "Fear thou not; for I am with thee: do not be dismayed; for I am your God: I will strengthen thee; yea, I will help thee; yea, I will uphold thee with the right hand of my righteousness."

An elderly pastor who lived nearby had a soldier friend escort him down the street to visit the Bishop's wife and me. As the day wore on rumours increased about the gravity of the situation. One of our old guards who watched the premises at night refused to leave us even during the day. When a lady arrived at our gate with her looted goods, he asked her what she wanted. The stranger said she was a relative of the Bishop's wife and wanted to speak to her. It was very obvious that the woman wanted to leave her ill-gotten loot with us so she could go back for more. The old night guard had never been to school, but he was very street wise. He answered the woman by saying he had worked at our home for a long time and never recalled her visiting the house before. He then told her, "Today is not a day for visiting, but a day for staying at home." With that he sent her on her way. It was his way of telling the unknown woman we wanted no part in what they were doing.

I believe his simple act kept us safe that day. We had asked God's protection and we had no intention of playing host to the devil's spoils.

By now the soldiers had stolen most of the vehicles in Kisangani. My Land Rover was still in the back yard, less than a stone's throw from the road. The high gates we had hung when we first arrived in Kisangani hid it. As I peeped out from behind the curtains I spied several soldiers walking past. I silently prayed. "Lord put a hedge around about us."

Just with that one soldier stopped and pointed at our gates saying to his colleagues, "Isn't there a Land Rover in there?" My heart sank!

His soldier friend replied, "A Land Rover? What would you do with it? Sure, you cannot even drive!" With that they were on their way.

I have been through many emergencies in Zaire and during days like this I mostly sit and read God's Word and find comfort and strength in it. I can assure you that reading the twenty-third Psalm when rebel soldiers are patrolling your street gives new meaning to the Psalm.

Later that same day I could hear two soldiers speaking very loudly on the road outside our home. Again I peeked from behind the curtains. Just then a lady rushed past and they stopped to ask, "Isn't that the home of the Bishop?"

"Yes," she answered, "but didn't you hear that he died in Kinshasa?"

They came again at her, "Well, what about his wife then?"

The woman did not hesitate with her reply, "Oh, her? She ran off into the bush as soon as the news of her husband's death came."

The soldiers seemed satisfied with that and were soon on their way. Meanwhile, we were rejoicing for yet another evidence of the Lord's goodness to us. On Monday night the shooting continued fast and furious. By this time the shops were totally empty of any goods. Everything had been stolen. Expatriates were leaving the area as quickly as possible. Again I was faced with the question if I should leave or not. It was a dilemma to know where to go, for Kinshasa was worse than Kisangani. Furthermore, I had no papers.

Without a permit to travel I felt I should stay for a couple more days. Because the shooting continued unabated on Monday night I trailed my mattress into the little storeroom which meant that stray bullets would have to penetrate at least two cement walls before hitting me. My neighbours sat up all night, but I could see no point in that so I lay down in peace and slept, even as the Lord had promised in Psalm 4:8. "I will both lay me down in peace, and sleep; for Thou, Lord, only makest me dwell in safety." From time to time I did waken to hear more shooting, but I was not unduly worried and soon fell back to sleep again.

I must honestly say there was such a sense of resignation to God's will that I actually prayed that if He wanted to take me home to heaven, I was ready to go.

Early on Tuesday morning the town was a little quieter, but by eleven o'clock the shooting was as bad as ever again. With so much gunfire I was sure they would be running out of ammunition before long. Many were praying that the gunfire would soon end. Stories began to filter in of many people who had either been injured or killed by stray bullets. By one o'clock that afternoon a fierce tropical storm began to sweep over Kisangani. Trees bent over in submission to the gale force wind and a thick darkness descended on the whole town. With the onset of the storm the shooting decreased markedly. That was because no one in Zaire likes to be caught outdoors in a rainstorm. The gathering storm had been a signal to the soldiers to cross the river and head out of Kisangani and back to barracks before the rain came.

The rain never did come. It was such a strange afternoon of weather with dark clouds hanging over the town and the wind persisting until late that night and yet there was not a drop of rain. It became evident to everyone that our God had delivered us and early Wednesday morning the prayer meeting was packed to the door as people gathered to praise God for how He had preserved us yet again through times of trouble.

21

Bicycles and Bibles in the Bush

The emphasis on democracy in Africa in the early sixties spread rapidly across the continent and threatened a lot of autocratic leaders and tyrannical regimes. Democracy also became contagious in the Protestant churches, where more autonomy and local control was desired, and at times demanded. No longer were they satisfied with the church programmes being governed by the Central Office of the Congo Protestant Council who worked out the Bible School curriculum. The Bible School Board of Directors assumed responsibility for their curriculum and decided to make their own decisions about the school's future.

I was present at a Board meeting when one of the older pastors was invited to speak about the history of the school. He recalled the good old days before independence and told of a pastor's conference back in 1955 and the great blessing it had been to everyone who had attended.

One of the younger men was present at the Board meeting and he picked up on the old pastor's comments and asked, "Why couldn't we have a conference for all our Bible School graduates? We could begin with those from Banjwade."

Some discussion followed the young man's suggestion, but representing the Mission, I was not at all enthralled by the suggestion. I pointed out the great difficulty of contacting our pastor graduates, some of whom now pastored churches up to seven hundred kilometres away. Besides being unable to locate the pastors, I also drew attention to the hardship some would face to travel to a such a conference. Many of them didn't even possess a bicycle and there was no public transport from most of the locations, indeed, in many places there were not even roads. To go along with the young man's suggestion would mean hosting more than one hundred pastors for approximately one week at a time when everyone was struggling to feed himself or herself. I therefore dismissed the suggestion as too idealistic, very impractical and one we should not even begin to think about.

Those present listened to both sides of the argument and decided to leave the matter and pray about it for one week and then everyone would return their reports. I went home to pray and put my case before the Lord, much as I had put it to the meeting. I remember summing it all up by praying, "You know Lord, this will never work out."

Sincerely in my heart I believed the whole thing was impossible and should not even be given much thought. Mail arrived each Wednesday and five days after that Friday meeting I received a letter from the UFM office in Northern Ireland telling me that someone had sent money which was earmarked "to feed the pastors at a meeting." I was taken aback and none too happy about this. However, when I went to pray I felt I had been wrong to pray as I had done. Still in the Lord's presence, the thought struck me that maybe He wanted us to arrange a reunion of the pastor graduates.

When we came together the following Friday it was unanimously agreed that we make plans for a conference in Banjwade in spite of the fact I had thought it would have been quite improbable and impractical. Banjwade was the chosen venue for the conference because the Bible School was there. Another reason for choosing Banjwade was that the River Lindi flows past the mission station and would allow some delegates to come by canoe. Besides, the river was the most convenient place for the delegates to bathe. Over one hundred former students and friends were invited to Banjwade from a seven-hundred kilometre radius. We still had to face the problems of how to feed them, where we would house them and how we were going to arrange transport. These problems seemed enormous to most, and impossible to me. However, once they started to make plans, things began to fall into place. One by one the impossibilities became feasible.

It was decided that each delegate would be responsible for getting to Banjwade and that each one should bring a live chicken. Some of those chickens travelled seven hundred kilometres in a small basket, which was tied to the back of the delegate's bicycle. Periodically the pastor popped corn into the cage to help his chicken survive the journey and keep her in good shape for the conference meals. Some pastors were on the road for two or three weeks and obviously forgot to feed their poor chickens for when they arrived there were more feather-covered bones than chicken!

Dr. Ken McMillan, a fellow UFM missionary working at Rethy which was nine hundred kilometres away, sent us two hundred kilos of dried beans. This was a real unexpected Godsend to us. Although beans are part of our staple diet yet they do not grow well in the Banjwade area, and the locals look on beans from Rethy as a real treat. We wondered how Dr. Ken was able to send so many beans just in time for the conference and discovered the Lord had worked in a strange way. A patient arrived at the Rethy Mission Hospital because he had been involved in an accident. When Dr. Ken treated him he found out that his patient was a truck driver from Kisangani, our home town. Ken knew our need for beans so he made a deal with the driver - his payment for the hospital treatment would be to transport beans to Banjwade. Even though it took the driver more than two months to arrive in Banjwade due to the bad roads, yet the food arrived in good time to supplement the chickens which had been brought from far and near.

Added to this timely provision, another amazing thing coincided with the conference. A Christian friend in Ireland sent money to purchase Bibles for all the delegates. Consequently we were able to give each one a new Bible for himself and four Bibles for elders or evangelists back in their home villages. Other monies were sent in from various sources for the special convocation of pastors and with this we were able to purchase new bicycles for the most needy pastors. Dr. Gordon Molyneux, a former UFM missionary to Congo, came from England to give the daily Bible readings, which rejoiced all our hearts. Bible teachers, Ted Witmer and Edner Jeanty, two UFM International missionaries from Bunia Theological Seminary, led various seminars.

The day at conference began at 6.00 a.m. with prayer in the church. By 7.00 a.m. one hundred men made their way to the river for their wash. I had my 'bath' in the little mud bathroom near my home. We were back in church by 8.00 a.m. for community hymn singing and Gordon's Bible study. For one hour each morning we feasted on the life of Nehemiah and his practical outlook on the Lord's work. We heard how we needed to learn from Nehemiah's attitude to the work that God has committed to us.

At 9.30 a.m. the current students' wives pounded on drums to summon all delegates for breakfast. This usually consisted of corn porridge, freshly made doughnuts or fried cassava. There certainly was enough food to keep us going until the next meal which would be served at 4.00 p.m. At the morning sessions young and older trained pastors treated practical issues ranging from 'How to Develop God's Church; The Role of the Pastor's Wife in Today's Church; How to Lead a Bible Study; Practical Guidelines for Follow-up Work.' Gordon, Ted and Edner made their contributions in all of the discussions which were often lively and heart-searching.

Timely teaching was interlaced with vivid illustrations from real life situations in Zaire, one of which came up as the delegates were being taught 'Being Honest in Bookkeeping.' The government was still paying teachers' salaries and they had an arrangement that each month an amount would be placed in the Church's bank account to pay our teachers. Already the government was many months in arrears with these payments and there were many related problems, especially in communication from the civil servants at the Education Department.

A young man who had been raised in our church had recently returned from Kinshasa with many certificates and diplomas for accountancy. Many of our church leaders were keen to employ him, but others of us had reservations. One question that loomed in everyone's mind was, "If he has such good qualifications why did he not secure a job in the capital where employment was much easier to obtain than in Kisangani, and better paid too?" Notwithstanding some reservations, the church put him in charge of the 'teachers' account" at the bank. Besides having power of attorney at the bank there were other signatories to the account thereby safeguarding the money.

During the second month of his employment the monthly money was withdrawn at around midday and he began the usual calculations to allocate the appropriate amount to each teacher. Two hours after he started the calculations he complained of feeling unwell and was unable to continue his work. For security reasons the money was normally stored at another location and he promised to deposit it there on his way home. Unknown to anyone at the education office he had already made plans for a high speed canoe to speed him down river from Kisangani towards Bumba. Because he lived alone no one noticed his absence from town until the next morning when he didn't turn up for work. His fellow workers checked at his home where neighbours informed them that he had not been there the previous evening.

Suspicions were aroused and the worst fears confirmed when they discovered the school's safe-deposit box was empty. Every one at the office and church was numbed to think that the 'qualified accountant' had 'wiped their eye.' During the next few weeks searches were made in every direction without any success. Every day different reports came in of him being seen in different areas.

The prayer meetings, which followed this incident, were very interesting. Many of the unpaid teachers cried to the Lord for help. "Lord you know this is your money and we know that you will care for us." Others prayed that God would work in the culprit's life. The accountant had presented all the outward appearances of a good Christian young man, but now so many people were disillusioned by him and felt that God was even more disappointed than they were.

A few weeks passed before news arrived from Bumba, seven hundred kilometres away, that the man had been caught trying to purchase several fields and houses and had been arrested. Church delegates were dispatched post-haste to bring the necessary charges against the offender and try to recuperate the money, if there was any left. Within days we heard that the thief was very ill and one week later we learned that he had died.

The incident made a deep impression on the people in Kisangani. Many were touched and trusted the Saviour because of the impact of the whole saga. When the story was told to the delegates at the conference there was a very long and sobering silence. They recognised that God is sovereign and we dare not play with Him. The teacher pressed home his point to the delegates, "No matter where your little village is, and no matter how dark your little hut may be, be sure God is watching you. This man reaped what he had sown and so will we."

The conference continued for seven days and many of these pastors considered it to be a dream come true, especially those who lived in isolated villages where they had no opportunity for fellowship with other pastors. One pastor told of how the conference was the first teaching he had received since leaving Bible School eighteen years earlier.

Besides the teaching seminars, a large part of the time was spent profitably listening to the difficulties other pastors faced and sharing how some had overcome the same problems. We in the Mission's central office gained a new insight into how we could best help these pastors.

Some years earlier, friends in the Broughshane district had provided me with a small generator. The generator was a great blessing in the evenings at the conference for it not only provided good light, but it also allowed us to show some Christian films. Besides the conference delegates, crowds of village people also arrived for our open-air cinema. Just at that time 'The Jesus Film' had been produced in Swahili and by popular demand we had to show it several times during that week. People had not been used to electric light in the evenings so the light enabled them to stay up later. Some said they thought 'there was no night' during that week.

The only sad note about the conference was that the man who first suggested having it, Rev. Safiko Amboko, became ill a few weeks before the conference began and was unable to attend. Visiting with him on our way to the conference he reminded me of Simeon in Luke's Gospel when he said, "God has answered my prayer in allowing the pastors to be together for the conference." In His sovereignty, God called Rev. Amboko home on the Friday evening of the conference week.

By Monday of the next week most of the pastors were again on their bicycles and facing the long journey home. They were returning to their home churches happy and refreshed from all God had done for them during the conference. Others delayed their departure for it would take them up to three weeks to arrive home so they wanted to purchase supplies in Kisangani, which for them was a big city. Some had received new bicycles and were glad to be pedalling their way in style while others had to replace tyres and brakes. For the next two weeks my house looked like a bicycle repair shop.

By the end of four weeks all of the pastors had gone whether by bicycle, on foot or by dugout canoe. The departure corresponded with a time when the political situation in the country was becoming more and more tense. Later we discovered that the last man arrived home on the day that war broke out again in Zaire. Who can doubt the Lord's timing and protection?

22

Making Our Lives Count For God

In 1997 a bloody revolution ousted President Mobutu who had reigned autocratically over an unsteady country for thirty years. A new regime under President Kabila was in place and Zaire reverted to being known as the Democratic Republic of Congo. During this transitional period it was necessary for missionaries to leave the country again, but it was only for a short time and soon life was back again as normal as life can be in Kisangani.

I arrived back in early July 1997, just in time to see many of my students graduating from Banjwade Bible School. I had only been in the country three days when we made the sixty-four kilometre trip from Kisangani to Banjwade, which took almost four hours. Everywhere we went new soldiers were in evidence as they manned road barriers and imposed many new controls on transport. On the day before the graduation service in Banjwade, which was to be on Sunday, ten of us who made up the jury for the exams, plus the driver, packed into my Land Rover. We had only gone eighteen kilometres out of Kisangani when we were confronted with the first barrier. A young soldier, no more than seventeen years of age, approached displaying all the military hardware he might need for a battle. He spied me in the car and immediately began to ask many questions about this 'white woman.' He thought I was a reporter or from one of the observation groups that visit Africa frequently.

He started to ask a whole series of questions about me, ranging from my nationality, the purpose of my visit, who had sent me and by whom I had been invited. There were many other questions to follow, but he used Swahili and I understood every word he spoke. Finally, the driver said, "You may ask her all of these questions; she understands Swahili."

I greeted him politely in Swahili. He was devastated that I had understood all this harsh questioning and without waiting for me to answer one of his questions, he quickly turned and walked toward the barrier. He would have known without a doubt that we were church people and he realised that he was out of line asking us such questions.

That incident started alarm bells ringing in the ears of our church leaders. If I was to continue teaching at Banjwade then I would have to travel this road weekly and come up against the numerous road-blocks and the soldiers that manned them. They judged that my life was not safe in doing that so they assigned me to remain in Kisangani to look after the young people's work.

The young people's seminars were proving very popular in Kisangani and became even more so when the planning committee decided that the December seminar should be residential. I could never imagine cramming one thousand young people into the church on Saturday night and then accommodating them during the weekend. However, the committee was autonomous and the national committee members were sure they could make it happen. They planned that the young people would arrive at the large central church on Saturday morning before 8 a.m. and activities were planned through until midnight. The men would sleep on the floor at the rear of the church and the ladies also on the floor at the front of the church and a guard of deacons were delegated to sleep in the middle!

By 8.00 a.m. on Sunday, the last week in 1997, all the young people had taken their places in a 'tidied-up' church for the morning worship service. It was a memorable day with well over two thousand voices giving thanks to God for His guidance and guardianship during the previous year. None praised God more than those young people who had been challenged on Saturday to 'make their lives count for God' in the coming days.

Not many weeks later opportunities arose for teaching God's Word to other young people. Over six hundred 'boy soldiers' had been moved to a new camp near Kisangani and six of our young people were prompted to ask the captain, "Could we teach these young fellows God's Word each week?" The boy soldiers ranged in age between ten and fifteen years. The captain gave official permission and that Thursday afternoon six frightened, but zealous young people and another leader and myself made our entrance into that army camp. We were all apprehensive about the reception we might receive and whether many officers might be present. We need not have worried, for only soldiers turned up and we were given excellent attention. We made a gentle beginning as we shared God's Word with them. From the very beginning it was evident that some of these boys had a little background of Christian things. They not only received the Word, but agreed that we should meet in their compound every Thursday evening and Sunday morning.

On the next Sunday we arrived at 7.00 a.m. to discover two hundred young soldiers had also turned up at that early hour for the service. These boys were all clad in a uniform of shorts and tee shirts, even though most of them were bare-footed. We not only marvelled that so many had voluntarily come to our meeting, but found there was such a hunger for God's Word. In the ensuing weeks we became a 'life-link' with normal life for these young soldiers. Most of their time was spent parading behind the high wire fence which surrounded the camp. Hunger, sickness, loneliness, frustration, stared at us in that camp every time we went for another meeting. It was encouraging to observe that the teaching of God's Word was already meeting some of the young men's needs.

On our second visit to the camp a young boy came to tell me something which was really a request. "Back home," he said, "in my village my father read God's Word to us every night before going to sleep. I don't have a Bible here. Could you please get me one?" As we chatted further it became evident that he was one of the few boy soldiers who could read and write. Next week I tucked a Bible into my large sack to slip to the soldier boy at a quiet moment. We were permitted by the authorities to distribute Bibles, but if I had openly given one away then all six hundred fellows would have been wanting a Bible. That would have been great, but was not possible at that time as we had a limited supply of Bibles.

On our next visit I looked for the young man after the meeting, but I could not find him and was sorry and blamed myself that I had not taken his name. I knew my description of him would explain who he was. Besides having a large scar on his left cheek, I remembered him telling me he was from the Rwandan border region. I asked for him at the camp from one of his fellow soldiers who told me, "Oh that is Yakobo. He died yesterday." I was shocked, but as the months went on stories similar to this followed a familiar pattern and we were to see many others suffer the same fate as Yakobo in future days at that camp.

With each week that passed, God's Word was changing the lives of young soldiers. When we had been teaching for nearly two months we gave each boy soldier an opportunity to earn a Bible for himself. Experience had taught us not to give Bibles away freely. They were better respected and cherished when a person paid for them or earned them. All these boys needed to do was to learn and repeat correctly ten of the Bible memory verses we had taught them.

We made a conservative guess that perhaps fifty or sixty of them might be able to learn these Scriptures and gain a Bible. Accordingly I reserved about sixty Bibles which I could afford to give away. I was taken aback the next week when I discovered rows and rows of these boys waiting to say their memory verses. Remembering I only had sixty Bibles, we had to be strict with corrections and only those who quoted the verses without a mistake qualified. I was penalised, for the exercise cost me over one hundred and eighty Bibles, three times the number I had estimated. Thereafter, whenever we passed by the wired fencing around the camp we could see small groups of boys reading the Bible together.

The lessons we gave to the boys ranged from 'The Miracles of Jesus' to 'The Life of Joseph.' When we got round to teaching an abbreviated study on the life of Moses the pastor finished off the meeting by inviting the boys to be like Moses, "Turn from your wicked ways and ask God to use you in this life." He continued, "If you want to take this step just wait behind after this meeting ." After he prayed, not one soldier left his place. The pastor, a Lingala speaker and not too confident in Swahili, asked me to explain to the boy soldiers what he had said. Because I learned Swahili before learning Lingala, my Swahili was easily understood so I explained and extended the invitation again. This time I suggested if they wanted to talk to us about God becoming the Master of their lives that they meet with us below a tree a little distance removed from where we stood.

All two hundred moved as a block and began to find a place in the shade of the tree I had indicated. I began to question if they understood what they were going for. We were faced with a dilemma and were not sure what to do. It was almost time for the curfew and we were nearly three kilometres from home, yet these boys were asking to talk with us.

I joined with the leaders for a short prayer to ask wisdom, after which we decided that the boys' questions were more important than the curfew so we would stay. We spent two hours praying and weeping together as one by one these young soldiers sought forgiveness through the Lord Jesus Christ.

As we spoke to them we learned what had triggered this mass response among the boys. When the young soldiers heard that Moses killed an Egyptian and hid the body and yet God was able to forgive and save him, they saw what Jesus did for them on the cross. Every one of those boys recalled the atrocities in which they had been involved during the brutal war so they seized the opportunity to get right with God. It was very moving to hear them call on God with broken hearts and confess their sins to Him. Our joy was abounding and even more so when God protected us on the road during the curfew for we did not meet any soldiers at roadblocks as we made our way home.

Over the next five weeks we had great pleasure, teaching these new converts when we met with them before or after the regular meetings. Many of them developed very quickly in their spiritual lives and they formed a choir of more than fifty voices.

Special permission was given to them to attend our large central Church service one Sunday morning where they sang and testified of what the Lord had done for them. As one young boy recounted his story there was not a dry eye in the whole congregation.

Early in August, just a short time after the young soldiers visited our church, there was another outbreak of war. Kisangani was under threat and it was being announced on radio that the rebel army was marching towards the city. Many more army personnel were needed to fight off the attackers.

These young boys were armed once more and put on the streets to defend the city. When Kisangani was invaded there were fierce battles all over town and hundreds of dead bodies littered the streets. Many of them were the young men we had led to faith in Jesus Christ.

Heaven will be a wonderful place, especially if you are going there from Congo. We will meet these young men in heaven and rejoice with them that a few young people had the courage to speak to the young soldiers about 'making their lives count for God'.

13

Strawberry Jam and Tears

War brought very severe consequences to every town. After the terrible atrocities of the mid-sixties when plantation settlers, business people, government officials and missionaries were abducted, abused and some massacred, traders were slow to return to Zaire. However, over the years they slowly came back and began to build up their businesses again. After thirty years of relative peace, political unrest began to take its toll and several businessmen had to abandon their shops and flee with their families. For those of us who stayed it meant that there were fewer and fewer European goods available in places like Kisangani.

National businessmen replaced many of the European merchants, but most of them did not have contacts in neighbouring countries such as Kenya and South Africa to import foreign goods. Those who did manage to import food and materials had to pay a very high price for them, which put imports beyond the reach of the ordinary people. Furthermore, with fewer expatriate workers in the country, the demand for foreign goods was also reduced and this was especially true when it came to imported foods.

Kisangani had an abundant supply of pineapples, bananas and papaw so we always had plenty of fresh fruit. While we thoroughly enjoyed the wide variety of tropical fruit, it was a treat to be able to buy a pot of strawberry jam that had been imported from England or South Africa. I will never forget the day I received a pot of jam someone in Kenya kindly sent me for Christmas. It was a touching treat! Because many visitors passed through my home, I had to keep the pot of jam well hidden at the back of the cupboard for those evenings when I was all alone. It was on those nights I treated myself to a piece of Kisangani bread and imported strawberry jam for my evening meal. I could make that jam last for months!

Just before Easter 1998 I was in one of the small shops buying bread when I noticed that they had some strawberry jam from Kenya, but it was over £4 per small jar. At such a price there was no way a Ballymena woman was going to part with that amount of money for a little drop of jam. I must say I was tempted, but I knew that what I had at home would last me for another week at least.

On Easter Saturday we were having a young people's rally and as the young people gathered in their hundreds early in the day, a young fellow came to see me. He had a small package wrapped in a piece of dirty paper. He said that his mother, who lived in a village about fifty kilometres away, had sent it to me. I put the parcel aside and at break time in the afternoon I opened it to discover the lady had sent me two eggs, some money and a letter. The letter read as follows:

"You will not remember me, but several years ago I came past your house for a drink of cold water. We chatted together and I told you I was moving house to another village and you gave me seeds for my garden and some money to buy oil and soap. God has blessed my family and me and we are very happy here. This year we had a good harvest and I am sending you my tithe money and want you to buy something for yourself. Do not give it to anyone else. You may want to buy yourself a nice pot of jam to eat with your bread."

I was astounded. I had to reread the letter to make sure it was true. I had just finished my first pot of jam that morning and here was God caring for me in a lovely way again. Sometimes when we read, "He careth for you" we tend to think that it is only in times of trouble or difficulty that He cares instead by continually showering His blessings on us day by day. He knows all our needs and desires, even though we may never voice them, and answers those inaudible and unexpressed wishes in ways that we could never imagine. His timing is always perfect.

The new area governor was working hard on repairing the Ituri Road and had mobilised all the local male population to work on the stretch of road leading to their local market. This thoroughfare had been deteriorating for years and meant that vehicles found it impossible to travel on. The two hundred and sixty-two kilometre trip from Kisangani to Bafwasende took anything up to three weeks on the bad road. Many people followed the progress reports of the repairs on the road on the local radio network, not least the Christians at Bafwasende. They had hoped for years for a visit from the church leaders in Kisangani but knew that the state of the road made that impossible.

Now that the workers had started to repair the road the believers in Bafwasende sent frequent messages on the two-way radio asking, "When are you planning your trip for Bafwasende?" I was not too enthusiastic about driving my twelve-year-old 'tied-together' Land Rover that sort of distance with ten pastors on board. I had not the heart to tell them I did not want to go so tried to avoid giving them a date for a visit. Reports were broadcast that the workers were now working between 240 - 250 km. With this news the invitation from the Bafwasende Christians became more pressing. "Please give us a definite date so we can plan the programme." they requested again.

Now I felt cornered and had to set the date for two weekends ahead by which time the workers would have arrived at Bafwasende. I could only see many justifiable reasons why I should not go on this visit. Special repairs were needed to the vehicle yet everybody wanted to travel with me. Try as I would, it was hard to convince more than fifty people who told me their good reasons why they 'needed to go to Bafwasende', that there was no room for them in the vehicle.

"You must teach seminars here as we have invited the young people," was the message they sent the day before we left. That meant preparation had to be done late into the night before we left at 6.00 a.m. next morning. We did not get away as planned for a faithful church member had died and that delayed our start, but as it turned out, it was in God's good time. That morning I received a radio message from Ireland that a dear friend, Rosetta Keefe, had died suddenly. Our delay allowed me to spend time to share in the grief of the local family and gave me opportunity to weep for Rosetta's family in their grief. I was also able to recount and give thanks to the Lord for all the help that Rosetta had been to me. She was the person who had encouraged me to go to the Berry Street Christian Endeavour group where my missionary interest had been nurtured. She was a faithful supporter and prayer partner of God's Work in Congo.

By nine o'clock we were on the road and even though we were three hours late, the folks along the road were so glad to see us. News of our trip had spread along the highway and many were waiting for us to give gifts of bananas, boiled eggs, cooked chicken and rice. We made good progress on the new road and after one hundred and forty-seven kilometres we stopped at Maganga to confirm that we would be there on the next Sunday evening to conduct a seminar for them on Monday. I had my own thoughts on that one as I had been to Maganga before. They were the people, who when revival broke out further up the road in 1952, said it was not of God, but of the devil and so closed the door to revival in their area. Since then teaching in Maganga had always been a nightmare. Few attended and even fewer listened or took part in the sessions. However, we had prayed that the Lord would open the door to conduct a seminar in Maganga so we would have to go ahead with it even though I had my own thoughts.

On our way through Boyulu we were able to meet with Rev. Magundi Paul with whom I had a special word. When I had been evacuated out of Congo and had gone home to Ireland I met an elderly lady at a meeting one snowy evening. Only the bravest Christians dared risk the elements that night to attend a missionary meeting. As I prepared to show slides of Congo this kindly lady started to ask me about where I worked. When I told her it was Congo she said, "That is in Africa, isn't it?"

I confirmed that her geography was right. The lady went on to explain that she had prayed for a man in Africa for over thirty years, but could not remember the name of his country. No matter how many questions I asked about the nationality or location of this friend her only answer was, "He is from Africa, love. That is all I know."

"Africa is a very big continent!" I answered and continued to set up the equipment. As I did so it struck me to ask the lady an improbable question, "What is the name of the man for whom you pray?"

When she answered "Magundi Paul", I almost collapsed for I was going to show a slide of his family in the presentation that I was about to give. I inquired how she had heard of Magundi Paul and she told me that many years earlier his picture appeared in a mission magazine and God had put it into her heart to pray for him and she had continued to do so since that time.

Magundi Paul was a faithful servant of the Lord and no doubt part of this was due to this lady's prayer support. All who serve the Lord know the value of faithful prayer warriors who often do the 'real work'. We certainly could not continue in His service without them.

When we arrived in Boyulu I went to see Magundi Paul and his family. This servant of God was deeply humbled and emotionally broken when I shared with him about this unknown lady who had prayed for him for so many years. He went on to say what a glorious place heaven will be when we shall meet up with God's children from around the world and in the eternal tabernacles of glory, friends shall greet friends who made an impact upon their lives on earth although they had never met.

Late that same evening we arrived in Bafwasende where hundreds, if not thousands of people welcomed us. I do not know where they all came from. By nine o'clock that evening we took our customary places around the camp fire and one after another was given the opportunity to share something from God's Word. I retired at about midnight, but the singing was still going strong at that late hour.

The prayer meeting at 6 a.m. was packed, as were the seminars which continued from morning to evening. The theme of the seminar was 'Setting Up a Christian Home' the topics of which included, "Asking God Who my Life's Partner Should Be"; 'Christian Parents Raising a Family.' These young people had never heard anything like this before and their comments were interesting; "You mean I don't need to run away with a girl to avoid paying the expensive dowry that her family is asking for her?" "You mean that Christian parents should not look on their daughter as a means of becoming wealthy through her dowry? Is it more important that she marries a Christian boy who will help train their children in God's ways?"

All this was evidently new teaching to these believers and was impacting their lives. When we came to the final topic, 'Lord, I Want to Follow You With All My Life,' it was followed by a time of private and public prayer which was mingled with much weeping and rejoicing. We took time to speak with many who were broken and asking such questions as, "How can I put right the wrongs I have done? I ran away with my wife and have never paid her dowry. What can I do now? I'm living with this girl and we're not married. I want to be right with God. What should I do?"

By the time we had listened and counselled dozens it was another late night, but a very happy one. Quite a few people had been converted, backsliders sought forgiveness and put things right with God. As I lay on the grass mattress in my mud hut that night, I thought, *Thank you Lord for winning over my hesitation and making me come to Bafwasende. What would have happened if I had continued to refuse?*

Sunday was the first graduation service of their newly built Bible School and it was a great day of rejoicing and praise. The church was not able to accommodate all who came so we decided to meet under the shade of the trees outside where thousands swarmed around for the service. Even government officials, who were in town to oversee the road repairs attended the meeting. God's Word was faithfully preached and again people sought the Saviour.

On Sunday afternoon we left Bafwasende and headed back to Maganga, the spiritually dry and barren place we had briefly stopped at on our trip to Bafwasende. We had to halt and say farewell to the Christians who had gathered to meet us on the road at Boyulu. Magundi Paul was amongst them and gave me a small gift to send to the lady prayer-partner in Ireland. I had a peep into the bag to see what he was sending to our friend. Ten fresh eggs lay at the bottom of the bag.   It would be impossible for me to send those fresh eggs home to Belfast, but Magundi was just so happy that he could say thank-you for the good news of a prayer partner.

The sun was setting as we pulled into the mission station at Maganga. The new church leader who had been appointed just a couple of months earlier led hundreds of people who had turned out to greet us. I recognised the new leader and was glad to see him. Some years previously I had encouraged and helped him go to Bible School. That first evening as we talked together he said, "Maizie, I know the history of this place, but God always has the victory." His sincerity was evident as he continued, "Since I have taken up this position we have been concentrating on prayer and many of us are praying that the Lord will break into our midst."

I didn't sleep too well that night thinking over what the young man had said. I knew I had my own views about the hardness in Maganga, but I believe God was speaking to me about the prejudices I had raised in my heart. It seemed as if the Lord was saying, "Maizie, do you believe that I can work in this place too? I am the LORD."

In my mind I wrestled with the thought of what God might do and whether I really believed it could happen here. I had changed my views by morning and was now looking forward to our seminar and wondering what would God do that day?

The church was packed for the start of the programme. We planned on teaching from 7 a.m. to 4 p.m., but at 6 p.m. we were still going strong. The people at Bafwasende had been very attentive, but these spiritually hungry believers were far more so. During the teaching sessions no one moved. If a baby cried there were frowns of disapproval all around. The people hung onto every word being taught. It was not only easy to teach there, but a pleasure too. God was changing people's lives and during the day many wept their way to the foot of the cross for forgiveness.

In my heart I was saying, "Lord, please forgive my unbelief."

By midnight I was back in my home thrilled at all God had done that weekend. Not only was I happy that the Lord prevailed and I had gone on the trip, but also that He had changed so many lives. As a matter of fact I was almost convinced that we really needed to make a return visit to Bafwasende and Maganga to teach more about the Word of God.

It wasn't to be. The *very next* morning an announcement was given over the radio, "War has broken out again in Congo". Rebels were using the road on which we had travelled back to Kisangani. They were heading toward our town, but thankfully, we arrived back just in time and before war had caught up with us. God's timing is always perfect and we proved that we can be comfortable in His planning and be content to go His Way.

24

God's Word is Our Rock

When a new president came to power in the Democratic Republic of Congo in 1997 the church was blessed with a period of peace after the unrest and hostilities of the previous few years. However, that peace was short lived. On 2nd August 1998, news arrived of another outbreak of war in Goma, which is in the eastern region of Congo. There had always been political rumblings in Goma, but as news began to filter through over the next few days, we realised the situation was a lot more serious than just political rumblings. We learned that rebels from Uganda and Rwanda were travelling north towards the Joint Mission Hospital at Nyankunde. Two-way radio operators who lived in the proximity of the main road from that region confirmed this news.

When I talked with Colin and Wynnonah Porter, our UFM missionaries, and Cathy Murray, a medical student doing a six-week elective in Nyankundi, it became clear they would have to move from the area. As their senior missionary colleague, I advised them to leave with the other missionaries who were heading for the Ugandan border to the North.

The days of uncertainty continued and for several days we were in constant radio contact with various missionaries. The contact ended when the missionary community in northern Zaire crossed the border into Uganda. They assured me of their prayers as we said our good-byes over the airwaves. They left me with Numbers 6:24; "The Lord bless you and keep you; the Lord make his face shine upon you and be gracious to you. The Lord turn his face toward you and give you peace".

It was then that I felt very much alone. I realised for the first time that all my colleagues with whom I had been sharing news over the past six turbulent days had gone. I would have no more contact with them and there were no other missionary colleagues with whom I could share what was happening. Also, the MAF personnel had left with the other missionaries. This meant that the e-mail system, which they had installed to facilitate contact with the outside world, now ceased to exist.

When I turned the radio off for the final time it was then that the thought hit me *I'm on my own.* It was early afternoon and when I returned to my house for lunch I picked up one of the many books that missionary colleagues had left with me over the years. It was *Day by Day by Vance Havner* and the date was 8th August. As I ate lunch I started to read the devotional and the very first verse seem to pop out from the page at me, *alone; and yet I am not alone, because the Father is with me.* (John 16:32). I could not believe what I was reading and yet there were tears in my eyes as I realised it was the Lord saying to me, "It's all right, I'm right here with you, I know all about you."

When I continued to read the little commentary that followed the verses, my teardrops turned to a stream of salty tears coursing down my cheeks. I had an assurance that, in a special way, the Lord was going to protect me from the approaching war.

In Kisangani rumours were rife about how close the rebels were to the town. Planes had already stopped flying and many locals were hiring canoes with outboard motors to take them seven hundred kilometres down river where they hoped to secure another flight. I did not feel that I should follow them and the church leaders assured me that all would be well and I should not try to get out that way.

Tensions continued to rise in Kisangani and it soon became evident that there was going to be a confrontation of opposing armies in or near the town. Government soldiers marched through the town daily in a display of strength for the benefit of the local population. I remembered Psalm 118:8,9 "It is better to trust in the Lord than to put confidence in man. It is better to trust in the Lord than put confidence in princes." The Word of God gave me strength and my daily readings were a pillar of support. Many Christian nationals came to my home to share what God was also saying to them.

In spite of the impending threats, we continued teaching our various classes, but rumours continued to circulate that the rebels were getting closer to Kisangani. On Saturday evening it all happened very suddenly. When it began I was sitting outdoors enjoying the cool of the evening with my neighbours. Suddenly, there was a loud burst of gunfire from the direction of the army camp followed by a continuous exchange of shooting which confirmed our worst fears that the rebels had arrived.

The neighbours were shocked that I should even think of going to bed, but my reaction was "If anything happens to me I'm going home to glory and He can take me from bed the same as from a chair." I went to bed, but sleep was intermittent during the night.

As soon as dawn broke I was searching my Bible reading for that day to see what the Lord had to say to me. The devotions took me to Psalm 91 where verses five through seven struck home; "You will not fear the terror of night nor the arrow that flies by day, nor the pestilence that stalks in the darkness, nor the plague that destroys at midday. A thousand may fall at your side, ten thousand at your right hand, but it will not come near you." I read and reread those verses. I knew that as long as I stayed indoors during the day the soldiers would not come near me. My house is at the roadside and from behind the closed curtains I watched as hundreds of soldiers ran up and down the road using their automatics to shoot into the air and frighten the town's residents.

The sporadic shooting continued for three days and through all this time His peace filled my heart. My national Congolese colleagues were a great encouragement and their fellowship was rich, but the greatest encouragement of all came each day from God's Word. I have used the book 'Daily Light' for many years and every day it seemed the selected portions just fitted my situation on that day. One day when things seemed to overwhelm me, Daily Light offered; "Do not throw away your confidence; it will be richly rewarded; You need to persevere..." *(Hebrews 10:35-36).*

The fighting eased on Tuesday night, but at midday on Wednesday the bell from the Roman Catholic Church rang continuously and with great force. The unusual and continual peel of the bell shot alarm through the town and everyone was afraid of what it might mean. We found out that soldiers had entered the Roman Catholic Mission property and were looting all they could put their hands on. The sounding of the bell was to alert the faithful to come to the aid of the church and protect its property.

Very soon an elder and a deacon from our church arrived at my home which was less than a mile away from where the looting was taking place. I was glad to see them, but then they began to tell me the purpose of their visit, "We have come with some very bad news for you. Do you hear the chapel bell?" The Catholic Church was located on top of a hill overlooking the town and there was no way anyone would miss hearing the bells. The two friends continued, "The soldiers are looting and they have a list of what they plan to do today. Their first objective is to plunder the Catholic Mission, which they are doing now. They then plan to attack the Kimbanguist compound and your house is next. We have come to let you know."

After I listened to them I said, "I appreciate you letting me know, but it's not really my problem. It is God's problem. He brought me here and He will take care of me and I am in His care." They stared at me in silence and to save their embarrassment or shock I said, "Let's pray together." We did and then I escorted them to the gate, as they wanted to get home before the rioting started.

I watched them hurry off and then I turned back indoors. It seemed as if the devil whispered an insinuation in my ear, "Those elders must think you are super-spiritual after answering them in that fashion." I tried to dispense the thought of being pompous or presumptuous. My Bible was nearby and I opened it to read from where I had left a Bible marker after my last visit to the Scriptures.

The page fell open at Colossians 3:16 which I had underlined several years earlier. They were familiar words, but I read them again, "Let the word of Christ dwell in you richly as you teach and admonish one another with all wisdom, and as you sing psalms, hymns and spiritual songs with gratitude in your hearts to God".

Assurance flooded my soul and I knew He was in control. What I had said to the elders was not meant as rudeness and much less, bravado. God kept me in perfect peace during those hours and the soldiers never did come to my house that day, or any day. God had already given me His promise the day the soldiers entered Kisangani.

I am forever grateful for the fellowship and friendship shown by my national colleagues during those stressful days. Not one day passed without Pastor Begege cycling over six kilometres early in the morning and past all the soldiers, just to visit me. Instead of his usual greeting of "How are you?" He called out; "The angel of the Lord encampeth round about them that fear him."

During his visit we usually had a cup of tea and some bananas while we talked of God's goodness and protection for us in the current crisis. After prayer for God's continued safekeeping, Pastor Begege cycled six and a half kilometres back to his home. Because it was not advisable for me to go outdoors, I spent a lot of time preparing simple literature on a new duplicating machine that we had recently received. In this way I was able to print thousands of tracts during those weeks I was confined to home.

Because the situation was not improving, indeed it was becoming increasingly worse, the church leaders advised me to consider looking for a way to leave Congo. This was easier said than done for by this time there was no reliable transport. No planes were flying, to exit Congo by boat was impossible and the roads were not fit for travel. However, in spite of these apparent obstacles, my heart was at peace and I knew the Lord would open up His way in His time.

At this precarious time, a young Norwegian short-term missionary arrived from the bush and was quite naive about what was happening. He neither spoke French nor Lingala and consequently had little understanding of the political rumblings and local agitation. His concerned parents, who had been missionaries in Kisangani many years earlier, sent and asked if I would take him with me wherever I was going. However, the young man was independent and it was good to see his faith grow leaps and bounds in the couple of weeks he spent with us.

One day we heard that a plane was taking off from Kisangani and we wondered if we should try and secure a place on it. We heard the plane belonged to the rebel soldiers. That morning I had been reading in Isaiah and came upon a most appropriate verse; "But you will not leave in haste or go in flight."

Ten minutes later the young Norwegian friend arrived and said, "I'm not leaving today for I read this verse in my quiet time this morning; *"But you will not leave in haste or go in flight."* It was not just coincidence that both of us had read the same Scriptures confirming that we should stay put.

A few days later we heard that a charitable British organisation was planning a relief flight into Kisangani and there would be a place for us when they flew out again. To secure the places we were instructed to contact the chief of the rebels. Our friend Pastor Aluta said he would go and see the chief for me. A few minutes later he returned dejected and said that I personally had to go and speak to the chief. I got a ride on the pillion of a motorbike to the large hotel where the soldiers were barracked. A ten-year-old boy who was holding an automatic weapon in his hands, with a plentiful supply of ammunition wrapped around his body, met me at the gate. He asked what my business was and when I told him I wanted to see the chief he said, "Mama, I'll give you ten minutes."

Because he had called me Mama I took the liberty of calling him son and said, "Son, if your big boss says I have to stay fifteen minutes what will you say?" He had no watch and I therefore knew there was no way he could measure ten minutes so I gave him a smile as he opened the gate and I proceeded through to meet the chief. I actually had to pass through five barriers before I got to the top man, and when I finally reached that far I was told he was in a meeting and was not to be disturbed. The solider said, "Come back at four o'clock."

It was now only 10.00 a.m. so I had to go home again. Just as I turned to go, the door opened and I heard a voice say, "Maizie are you still in Kisangani?" I looked back to see a man I had met many years previously. I recalled that his child had been very ill and I had given them a couple of Paracetamol tablets which helped the little one. At that time he held a position in President Mobutu's government, but now he had changed sides and led a faction of the rebel army.

I turned back to greet him and was taken aback when he gave me a hug and asked what he could do for me. I explained that I wanted to make a trip to Britain and was looking for a way to leave Kisangani. "No problem," he said, "come back in the afternoon and I will give you the necessary papers."

At four o'clock that afternoon the young Norwegian worker went with me to try and secure a place. Subsequently we were assured that the plane would arrive on the following Saturday, but confirmation could only be given twenty-four hours before the plane was due to arrive.

On Friday, I duly returned to the office to confirm our reservations as promised. It was then that I was told that the plane was delayed and would only come the following week. With yet another delay and plans frustrated, God's Word continued to be a great comfort with reassuring verses such as, "Cast your cares on the Lord and He will sustain you; Those who hope in the Lord will renew their strength; The Lord is with me; he is my helper; If God is for us, who can be against us? The Lord is with me; I will not be afraid. The God we serve is able to save us from it, and He will rescue us."

When I arrived back to my house after learning that the plane was not coming, a young boy arrived at my door with a radio message for me. An Iranian friend in Goma sent word to say he knew I was in Kisangani and that I should leave immediately as more fighting was imminent. He went on to say there would be a flight on Sunday afternoon and there was a place for me on that plane. He told me to be ready at 1.30 p.m. The boy who brought the message said he would be available to take me to the airport. I wondered if this was another door that the Lord was opening and an opportunity to exit from Congo.

Bright and early on Sunday morning I packed my small suitcase yet again. I read my Swahili Bible that morning and found this for my meditation, "Sit still my daughter, until you see how the matter falls." What could this mean? I am hoping to leave today Lord. Surely there will not be another delay? I reasoned these questions out before the Lord and yet I knew this was God's Word to me.

I went to the Sunday morning service at church and in my heart I was hoping to hear something different there. Quite often when missionaries are due to leave the country the pastor will offer them a verse such as, "The Lord will watch over your going out and coming in from this time forth and even forevermore." However, during the whole service not one reference was made to my planned departure. I was most disappointed. I hurried back home after church to catch a quick bite before the plane would come at 1.30 p.m. as had been arranged in the radio message.

Not long before the proposed departure time the boy who delivered the original message arrived at my door very apologetic. "I don't know how to say this," he said. "The government officials have taken over all the seats on the plane and there is no place for you. I'm very sorry, but perhaps there will be another plane later on in the week".

He was very embarrassed in giving me this information, but I assured him all was well and I had been half expecting that news. I went on to tell him of the Bible reading that morning, "Sit still my daughter…" He looked at me as though I had two heads and off he went.

Now that I knew I would not to be on that flight I wondered what God was working out for me, and how it would happen. That night gunfire continued to be heard all over town. Locked in the security of my house, I meditated on what the Lord was doing. Hebrews 10:35 clearly came to me again, "Do not throw away your confidence; it will be richly rewarded. You need to persevere." These words were still on my mind when I fell asleep that night. Even though the noise of sporadic gunfire in the town broke the silence of the night, yet I was able to sleep in peace knowing that my God was in control.

Early the next morning, shortly after 6.00 a.m. the same messenger boy was back on my doorstep. "What did you say to me yesterday?" he asked. I told him that I was a Christian and while reading God's Word I came on a verse that said, "*Sit still my daughter...*" I further explained how God by His Spirit showed me that verse was for me.

"Why do you ask?" I probed as he kept staring at me in amazement.

"That plane arrived yesterday," he said "and the fifteen passengers took off as planned. When the plane arrived at its destination the passengers disembarked and as they made their way to the terminal building fighting broke out. All of them were killed."

The boy was obviously stunned and I was shocked with the news. Again the Lord had protected me from a disaster and I was overcome with gratitude to Him. I continued in conversation with the young man and it was a great opportunity to share with him how God takes care of His children and, because He knew ahead of time what would happen to that plane, my way had been blocked.

For days the threat of imminent war in Kisangani was very real and the population lived in fear. Almost every day I was promised that a plane would be coming 'tomorrow.' On Wednesday I was assured of a flight on Thursday, but that was discounted early the following morning with another assurance that it definitely would come on Friday morning. I was told to be ready to travel at 6.15 a.m. With hesitant expectation I rose very early and got ready to travel. I was really excited this time for I had read, "Behold I set before you an open door and no man can shut it." I knew that today the plane would come.

At 6.15 news came through that there would be no plane. At first I thought the messenger was playing a joke on me, but it dawned on me the news was true. The church had already planned a day of prayer and fasting for the overall plight of the country, so leaving my packed suitcase sitting in the living room, off I went to the prayer meeting. Between 7.00 a.m. and 11 a.m. much prayer went up for the situation in our beloved Congo. Our church leaders were stranded in the capital; many people had fled to the forest where food was very scarce; no longer were there any supplies in our dispensaries and Bible School students were stranded far from their homes as they had gone on practical work during the school holidays. Many needs were before us.

At 11 a.m. there was a thirty-minute break and I decided to go home for a few minutes, only to be met by a bright yellow car on the road at my gate. Sitting on the bumper of the car were two soldiers, one with a rocket launcher and the other with an automatic weapon. I made inquiries from the man at our gate about what was happening and was told there was a man in the yard looking for me. The man at the gate didn't know who the visitor was or why he was at the house.

As I entered the house I recognised our visitor as the 'chief of rebels.' He greeted me with, "Maizie, where were you?"

"I was at the prayer meeting." I answered.

"Who were you praying for?" He quizzed.

"We were praying for you people, that you will soon settle the problems in our land." was my reply.

"Where is your suitcase?" he asked. I assured him that it was packed and ready for my trip, but wanted to know why he was asking me. "A plane has arrived from Uganda with supplies for the army. It is at the airport and they are waiting for you." he said.

"Oh, I need to take the Norwegian fellow with me too." I said.

"Well, find him quickly." he retorted. I soon sent someone to look for our young friend. "How are you planning to go to the airport?" the chief asked me. I replied that I did not know. I did know however, that I would probably lose my baggage between home and the airport because rebel soldiers lined most of the seventeen kilometre route and they would more than likely plunder what possessions I had, including passport and other important papers.

As if he was reading my mind, the chief looked at me and said, "Oh, come on and I'll take you out there."

Within ten minutes we were bundled into his bright yellow car with the two soldiers either side of us. The driver dropped the chief off at his hotel where another important officer joined us and soon we were speeding toward the airport. When the soldiers lining the road saw the yellow car they recognised it as belonging to their local commander and so we were saluted at every point. We felt God was treating us in style.

At the airport we were very well received by the military personnel and told that we did not need to pay for the flight. Soon we embarked on the forty-ton Russian Antonov aircraft. There were no soft seats on the aircraft, just benches along both sides of the huge transport plane. We took our places for the flight and soon we were airborne, evacuated from Congo on our way to Entebbe, Uganda.

Tears ran down my face as we looked below at Kisangani and the surrounding forest where so many of our friends remained in this war zone. Although it was necessary for us to leave Congo, yet I was saddened by the whole episode. I was also somewhat jealous that I was leaving the place where for six weeks I had known the Lord's leading and daily care at every turn.

25

In a Hurry

I was quite distressed that in leaving Congo in such a hurry, I had no time to say goodbye to my friends. At the same time, I knew that I could not afford to miss the opportunity God had provided to leave the hostile region. My Norwegian friend left for home while I travelled on to Kampala where Gary and Doreen Toews from MAF welcomed me to their home. They joined with me in giving thanks to God for how He had protected me and opened up an evacuation route.

When I finally arrived in Northern Ireland I learned that so many people had been praying for me during the six-week crisis. The Ballymena Presbytery had arranged special times of prayer on the Sunday that I failed to get a place on the plane on which all the passengers were killed. Again I could see how God is so great and was truly in control.

Before I left Congo my friends in Kisangani asked me not to forget their plight when I arrived back to Europe. Their one plea was for us to pray for them and to support them in whatever way possible. However, now that I was out of Congo, I wondered about my immediate future? I knew that the UFM worked in other fields and I contemplated going to one of those yet I knew that Congo held a special place in my heart. When I began to push doors to some of the other UFM fields I seemed to come up against many 'brick walls' and I had no peace or joy in contemplating serving the Lord elsewhere.

Even though there was no telephone system in Kisangani there was one satellite fax system still in operation. Internet also proved to be a big help as we tapped into the various news reports from government agencies. The arrival of Ugandan and Rwandan soldiers in Kisangani brought an escalation of the conflict as both armies competed to take control of the region.

In mid-August our church leaders left Kisangani on a 1600 kilometre journey to the capital, Kinshasa. They had been called there to attend the biennial meeting of all the Protestant National Church leaders of Congo. Kinshasa was still under the control of the Congolese government and this meant that the leaders were detained under a different jurisdiction and not able to travel back to the rebel-controlled area. To further complicate the situation, Bishop Assani, who was president of our UFM related churches, became ill while in Kinshasa and this brought added stress to his family and friends in Kisangani. Besides not being able to return home, he had precious little news of their welfare other than the daily radio reports of suffering in the Kisangani region and this further complicated his ill-health.

While still in Northern Ireland I received a call to try and help in the situation. This was much easier said than done. Passports are not easily come by in Congo and few people possess them. The only way to help Bishop Assani and the other three leaders to return home was for them to travel through Kenya to Uganda and then over the border to their region. Besides being a costly journey, it was also problematic. No airline would provide a single ticket for a Congolese passenger travelling to a destination outside Congo. Purchasing return tickets doubled the expense for they only needed to travel one way. Furthermore, travelling from the government-held area to the rebel-held area brought its own problems, but it also took months to obtain a passport and after that they still needed to apply for visas for Kenya and Uganda.

Two development workers, who had gone to Kinshasa for a seminar, accompanied Bishops Assani and Mehuma. As they were 'children of the church' I felt I had to help them get home to their wives and families. After we were able to procure their tickets through the Nairobi office the Kenyan embassy in Kinshasa gave them each a one-week visa. That meant we had one week to get them through Kenya.

Everything seemed to be going well. They had passports with current visas in hand so I travelled to Nairobi to await their arrival. After two weeks of the usual uncertainty that characterises most arrangements in Africa, I went to Nairobi airport to welcome them on the first leg of their journey home. I was so happy to see them all, but at the same time I got a shock when I saw how emaciated they were. Some of them were at least thirty pounds lighter than when I had last seen them in Kisangani over a year earlier. During that year away from home all of them were crammed into one room in Kinshasa and literally prayed for their daily bread. God answered their prayer when friends brought small amounts of food to sustain them. Their presence in Kinshasa had placed many families in difficulties as they tried to feed 'four extra mouths' on an already meagre budget. It was a miracle that they survived the conditions and God had surely protected them from danger.

When they arrived in Kenya we were excited for we knew they were halfway home. However, there were other hurdles to cross. They now had to work on the next leg of the journey and obtain visas for Uganda.

Accompanying our delegates on the flight from Kinshasa were the church leaders of the WEC fellowship of churches who also were following the same route to return home through Uganda. The president of their fellowship of churches had been one of my students at the Bible School in Bunia and was one of those who had washed dishes at Maizie's sink. Besides being glad to see them I was also happy to be able to help them.

Later that night at a Mission guesthouse, I was able to catch up on all the news from Kinshasa and what was happening on the government side of the entrenched conflict. Each of the seven delegates shared how God had protected them and provided for them, but it was very evident they were all eager to return to their families and churches.

Early next morning we completed the necessary forms and delivered these and the seven passports to the Ugandan embassy. We were told to return to collect visas and passports at 4.30 p.m. that same day. Having been assured that all would be well, we returned in good time to pick up the passports only to have our hopes dashed when they told us that the requests for visas had all been refused.

When visas were denied for Uganda I was left on the horns of a dilemma. I was responsible for seven delegates staying in a guesthouse in Nairobi, which costs money, and they were refused permission to return to Congo. The men knew they were in a predicament and we had a concentrated time of prayer that evening. Next morning I went to see the Ugandan Consul and tried to explain to him how impossible their situation was. He was adamant that these people, who had come from the government-held territory of Congo, should not return to the area held by soldiers from his country. Our discussion became quite heated and I assured him that I was not leaving his office until he permitted these church leaders to return to their homes. I argued with him that Northeastern Congo was their home region where their wives and children lived and how could he possibly refuse to let them go home. I had many official papers to back my argument, but they were in French and he only spoke English!

The Consul turned on me sharply and alleged that I had never helped Uganda in any way. Just then the Lord brought to mind my good friend from MAF, Gary Toews who was still working in Kampala. I told the agitated Consul that one of my 'family' was a pilot helping in relief work in Kampala. As if to try and call my bluff he demanded, "Who is he and what is his telephone number?"

I searched deep into my handbag and found my address book. It contained a mine of information and sure enough I was able to find Gary's mobile number. I feared he might be in the air as he flew every day, in which case we would not be able to contact Gary on his mobile phone.

The Consul took the number and dialled it. I heard someone reply to the call and soon the questions were being asked "Do you know Maizie Smyth? With whom does she work? Who is Bishop Assani? Who is Rev. Kibuka?" To each question he seemed to receive immediate replies and finally to Gary he said, "Thank you."

The Consul's appearance and expression noticeably changed as he looked across the table at me and said, "I will grant the visas."

While all this was happening several of the delegates were sitting in the waiting room, praying that God would intervene. He did. I found out later that when the Consul called, it had been the only day in two weeks that Gary had not been flying. God had it all planned.

The visas were issued and early next morning we caught a flight to Kampala. Now that we were in Uganda we discovered we had another major hurdle to cross. Their visas for entrance to Uganda indicated that they were in transit, but there was no flight available to take them to Kisangani. With time running out, we spent many hours trying to extend their stay in Kampala until a plane was available to fly them to Kisangani.

During this prolonged episode Bishop Assani fell ill again and we feared he might not reach home. We literally cried to the Lord for the next seven days. God was gracious to his dedicated, but aged servant and Bishop Assani recovered sufficiently to allow him to board the plane bound for his home. Before we parted at the airport he was so thankful that God had allowed him to return to his family again. He hugged me and said "I thank God for you, but I will never see you on earth again. We will meet in heaven." His prediction was accurate and he must have known his time was short. After a short period at home during which he was dogged by ill health, God called him home to his reward.

He had a long and fruitful life, but Bishop Assani's last days on earth were very difficult. He had lived through revivals and revolutions in his native land. He had often been threatened with death and yet was a tower of strength to missionaries and nationals alike when many of them were massacred for the sake of the gospel. Now at the end of his life he saw so many of his people still suffering all around him. He was a generous man who always wanted to help any one in need, even to the point at times of causing hunger to his own family. Bishop Assani could never say 'No' to anyone in need. Such refusal did not exist in his vocabulary.

On many occasions Bishop Assani tried to communicate with us about the needs of the medical dispensaries which were scattered throughout his region. Widows and orphans in the church were his special concern. I learned a great lesson from him early in my days in Kisangani. A widow who lived near the church became very ill. She had no connection with our church, but Bishop Assani often stopped by her house just to bid her time of day. During her sickness he frequently gave her a little money for food. One morning very early, he came to my home to tell me that the lady had died. She had no immediate family and so he instinctively knew he would have to bury her. He asked me to look at the meagre church accounts and see if I could find enough money to buy a coffin.

I had looked over those church accounts for many 'emergencies' and knew that there was no money available. I told the Bishop that there was nothing available. He looked at me and said, "Timothy was told by Paul to honour the widows. Surely Maizie, that is something we still need to do today."

Even though it was only the middle of the month he had already used up more than half of his small salary. He then instructed me to use the rest of that month's salary and part of next month's to buy that coffin. To bury the unbelieving widow meant that his family would go hungry because he wanted to obey God.

I broke down for I felt rebuked and embarrassed. I knew I had more money than he had, so I bought yet another coffin for a poor neighbour, but that morning I was taught a lesson in generosity by one of God's giants.

The Bishop's funeral was a great occasion of praise to the Lord for all that God had enabled His servant to do. Understandably, the Bishop's death was especially sad for his wife and children, but they, with us, share the confidence and blessed hope that one day we will meet him in heaven.

Although Bishop Assani's home-call left a great gap in Congo and especially among our congregations, yet the church had to move on. There was great frenzy among the people when they were called upon for an election to choose a new man to lead the church movement. Any sort of election is considered to be a great honour and when the church members cast their votes they unanimously elected Rev. Mehuma Huma Bolita, a younger man than Bishop Assani, to the position. Stability has not yet returned to Congo, but to this day, Rev. Mehuma Huma Bolita continues to lead the work of the Communaute Nation de Christ en Afrique in the Democratic Republic of Congo.

26

War and Want

The ominous dark clouds of war continued to hang over Congo as the battle front ebbed and flowed from month to month and opposing forces supported rival power bases within the country. Thousands fled their homes to the relative safety of the forests while many others were unmercifully massacred. The anguish and turmoil of those dark days exacted a very heavy toll on the population in Kisangani. Shortage of food and supplies was one of the devastating results of the conflict. People, and especially children, in the town were deprived of basic nourishment while those who had fled to the forest found it difficult to survive.

One of the contributing factors to the lack of food was that fewer people dug or planted in their gardens for fear of the passing soldiers who often plundered what crops they could find. The lack of fresh fruit and meat upset the diets of over 90% of the population. Malnutrition left the population vulnerable to all sorts of illnesses, which in turn put a strain on the local medical dispensaries and these were very soon depleted of medicines. Appeals arrived from the church in Congo for fresh medical supplies. However, not only did the church not have funds to purchase medicines, but no medicines were available in Congo due to the lack of river and road transport and whatever drugs arrived by plane were so expensive only the very rich could afford them.

We tried every way to keep the supply lines open and although at times it was nearly impossible, yet with the help of many generous friends, we were able to maintain our twenty-five dispensaries and thereby helped thousands of people in tragic times.

During all the time I was absent from the Congo I was able to constantly monitor the situation by tapping in to government and rebel news reports on the internet. Thousands of miles separated me from Congo, but I felt as if I was there with my friends in Kisangani during their suffering. Besides rallying prayer support for them around various churches, I longed to be able to do something practical to help them. I wondered if we could enlist support from churches to establish soup kitchens and food distribution centres in strategic areas to help relieve some of the hunger. However, I had to think about how we could go about setting up this programme and about who would manage it.

During a visit to Kampala in 1999 to deliver another batch of medicines for the dispensaries in Congo, I met up with several delegates from the Kisangani church to discuss the possibility of a food relief programme. Consequently, it was decided that we should look for help from some of the aid organizations who were working in Central Africa.

We also agreed that it was best to help promote the growing of garden vegetables, fruit and other crops in Congo. Under local supervision, the young people in the churches were encouraged to dig the gardens around the church buildings. On these church properties they planted soya beans, corn on the cob and other staple foods. We pledged to send in milk, sugar and salt. This simple programme saved the lives of so many children who might otherwise have succumbed to malnutrition.

The UFM board asked that while I was not able to return to the Congo, I continue to assist the Congolese church in all of these projects and other possible ways. In mid 1999, just when the UFM made their request, I received an appeal from Kisangani to help them provide new hymn books for our two thousand churches in their country. Their old hymnbooks were tattered and torn and to reprint in Congo made the price so prohibitive that the ordinary people could not afford them. Furthermore, the hymnals had been published separately in Lingala and Swahili and this created difficulties in some areas where not everybody spoke both languages.

Our friends at Every Home Crusade in Belfast said that they would accept the project of publishing a new hymnbook for Congo. I went about the task of compiling a new book containing French, Lingala and Swahili hymns, which could be used in all our church services whichever of the three languages were spoken. It was a mammoth project and without the help of Ernie Allen, Samuel Adams and the Every Home Crusade team, we would never have been able to complete the job.

It was a great day when seventy thousand new hymnbooks rolled off the press in Belfast and soon they were on their way to Kisangani. This major step brought great encouragement to the Congolese believers who were ecstatic about the new books. It also helped cement a bond between them and believers outside Congo, assuring them that other Christians cared for the Congolese Christians in their plight.

To co-ordinate the various programmes to which I was committed, it was necessary for me to travel to Kampala three or four times each year to meet with church delegates from the Congo. Besides consultation about the state and needs of the church in Congo, we spent two exhausting weeks securing medicines for the dispensaries, buying supplies for the Bible Schools and stocking up on powdered milk, sugar and salt for the food relief centres. In addition, we had to see to all the customs formalities, which could be very tedious and time consuming.

The delegates also brought piles of personal correspondence from my good friends in Kisangani. Many of these letters made personal requests for all sorts of items. One pastor wrote, "I have no shirt for Sunday church...could you please buy me one?" Another sent a piece of paper on which he had obviously outlined his children's feet and asked If I could go to the second-hand market and buy them shoes.

I tried to attend to as many of these requests as possible and after everyone else went off to bed I stayed up to write a personal reply to all the letters so that our friends could take them back to Kisangani on their return trip. Sometimes there would be as many as one hundred letters needing a reply, so that kept me busy through to the wee hours of the morning. I did not mind for this was my lifeline with those whom I loved dearly in the Lord.

Invariably, the majority of the letters asked us to send Bibles in Lingala and Swahili. I did not know where I could obtain Lingala Bibles in Kampala. English is the main language spoken in Kampala and Luganda is the tribal tongue of that region. In the city there are three Christian bookshops and when I visited each of them they had never even heard of Lingala Bibles. The outlook for purchasing them was very bleak.

It was a Monday night when I sat with the delegates in the cool of the evening outside the Anglican Guest House where we were staying. We discussed what still needed to be done in the remaining four days before they returned to Congo. During the discussion, one delegate asked if the Bible Society had an office in Kampala. I was not familiar with the city and could not give an answer so we inquired of others staying at the Guest House, but they also had no knowledge of the Bible Society in Kampala.

After breakfast and a prayer time next morning we decided to walk to a shop where we had been told powdered milk was being sold at a very competitive price. Even though it was still early, it was hot and sticky walking in the sun. After half-an-hour we were already feeling weary, undoubtedly the result of a series of busy days and very late nights, so we just ambled along through this unfamiliar part of town. As we approached the shop we noticed a large building on the other side of the street and above the entrance was a plaque which spelled out 'Bible House.'

We could hardly believe what we were seeing. We crossed the street and discovered that the building housed the headquarters of the Ugandan Bible Society. When we asked the receptionist if they had any Lingala Bibles she told us they never stocked them. I then asked to speak to the Director. She seemed reluctant to let us through to him and told us that his answer would be exactly the same as hers.

I told her that I wanted to ask other questions. She diffidently agreed for us to meet the Director whose office was on the next floor. As we climbed the stairs I asked Rev. Aluta, one of the delegates, to be our spokesman and I would interpret for him. It was a long time since I had been in Kisangani, but he had just arrived from there and would be able to give a better and more up-to-date picture.

The Director greeted us warmly and after the formality of introductions, Rev. Aluta launched into his discourse about Kisangani. He explained that although Congo was very much a war zone yet more people were attending church than ever before. However, Bibles were needed for the growing congregations. Speaking in Swahili, the Rev. Aluta began to tell the story of one man, a Muslim, who had been very opposed to the gospel and had been injured in a recent six-day battle.

Missiles and mortar bombs continued to rain down on Kisangani and made it impossible for the man to get any medical help. The nurse at our medical dispensary lived next door to him so he crawled from his mud hut to hers and asked for help. She was able to give him the needed treatment and over the next days took care of her patient. Through her actions she communicated to her neighbour the love of Christ and as a result the man trusted the Saviour. Not only he, but soon his family also understood what Jesus had done for them and they too trusted the Lord Jesus. However, no Bibles were available for this family so every morning while the nurse was at work she loaned them her Bible and then collected it again in the evening. Leaning across the desk toward the Director, Rev. Aluta added emphasis to what he was saying, "Doesn't that family need a Bible of their own?"

The Director was enthralled as the pastor continued to speak about Bible School students who had one Bible between three of them. He finished by asking if he could possibly place an order for us for Lingala Bibles. I translated the whole appeal into English and at the end the Director sat back in his chair and said, "I simply cannot believe what I am hearing."

He looked at Rev. Aluta and pointedly said, "Let me now tell you my side of the story. About two years ago I made an order for English and Lugandan Bibles. From the time an order is placed until it is delivered can take anything up to a year. After one year the consignment of Bibles finally arrived, sixteen tons of Bibles. They were off-loaded at the front of the building where I checked and signed for them. We moved them to our depot where we separated the cartons of English to one side and the Lugandan Scriptures to the other. On the outside of each carton there is a code indicating the language group contained in the box. In the process of separating the boxes that came we discovered we had thirty boxes which had a code we did not recognise. On checking the code we discovered the cartons contained Lingala Bibles. We had no outlet for them here in Kampala with the result I put them at the back of the store and they are still there."

I became so excited about what the Director was saying that I nearly forgot to translate the conversation for the pastor. My mind was racing ahead of him and I was wondering if I could afford to buy all of these Bibles? The Director leaned over to Rev. Aluta and asked, "Would you like to buy them?" The pastor and company were dumbfounded by what they had heard. We assured the man no mistake had been made for we believed this was God's miraculous provision.

We could hardly conceal our delight, but we did not have enough money to buy thirty boxes of Bibles so we told the Director we would return the next day, Tuesday. Although we didn't have enough money, a phone call to our very good friend, Mr. Edmund Norwood, Irish Secretary of UFM, soon sorted it out with the mission for me. The Director sold us the Bibles at a 20% discount and because he was so happy to be rid of them he agreed to transport them to the airport for us.

The flight to Kisangani was arranged for Friday, but we needed to deliver the precious cargo on Thursday. While the delegates finished their shopping in Kampala I decided to accompany the Bibles for the forty-kilometre ride to the airport. We started out early afternoon, but the truck had only gone about ten kilometres when the engine began to splutter, cough and then finally died. I sat by the roadside with the helpers for the rest of the day while the driver unsuccessfully tinkered at the engine. Finally, one of the helpers went to town and brought out another truck on which we all returned to Kampala with the cargo of Bibles because the Freight Depot at the airport had already closed.

I knew that the Freight Depot was infamous for goods being stolen and we half expected that many of our precious Bibles would not make it to Kisangani. The broken-down lorry made sure the consignment of Bibles never made it to the airport.

Early next morning I went with four other helpers and a driver to see if we could arrange for the embarkation of the cargo for Kisangani. When I met the plane's captain I told him we had arrived with the freight. He barked at me "We told you to come yesterday. Now you will have to go straight to the plane and load them yourselves."

The four helpers made short work of loading the shipment onto the plane. On the way back to town I marvelled at how the Lord had engineered our circumstances so that we never even ran the risk of losing a Bible at the Freight Depot.

I would just love to have been in Kisangani when the deputation and cargo arrived. There were scenes of rejoicing when the believers heard how God had miraculously provided Scriptures for them. In troubled times the Congolese Christians received so many assurances of how God cared for them in their plight.

27

Language and Literature

I am not a person who is easily frustrated, but I must confess that trying to organise and manage aid programmes at a distance brought a fair share of frustration. No matter how much help and how many supplies we sent to Congo we never seemed to be able to keep up with the needs of the people. Furthermore, I felt that I could have done so much more if I had been in Kisangani. However, with the passing of time I began to clearly see God's hand controlling and guiding my times. I had peace that I was to be based in Ireland for the meantime. We were also much encouraged when we learned that in the absence of missionaries, many pastors, evangelists and teachers were reaching others with the gospel. I recognised that God was asking me to be a back-up worker for them and was content to play this role.

Besides providing hymnbooks for Congo, our friends at Every Home Crusade in Belfast had been supplying us with quantities of Bible literature for many years. While in Ireland for the prolonged period I became more acquainted with the magnitude of their work as they produce Scriptures in over seventy languages and send them to over one hundred countries throughout the world. When I visited their factory in Belfast I was overwhelmed to discover they were printing three tons of gospel literature every day.

Mr. Ernie Allen, founder of the Revival Movement and Every Home Crusade in Ireland, is a giant of faith. His passion is for God, grace and the gospel. Although not a much-travelled man or a charismatic figure, yet for over sixty years his influence for God has touched millions of people all over the world. Over the years Ernie has seen the work develop and today a dedicated team of more than twenty workers under the leadership of Samuel Adams, strive to send out good quality Christian literature. I was surprised one day when I received an invitation to pay a visit to the EHC office to have a chat with Ernie and Samuel. The invitation provoked some speculation on my part of what they might have in mind.

When I met with Mr. Allen and Samuel they explained that they had received numerous requests for literature from various African countries, especially the French-speaking ones. They endeavoured to honour all these orders, but were concerned that they did not know who the recipients of the literature were and therefore wanted to know if I could possibly help them. Ernie Allen and Samuel asked if I would be willing to visit some of these African countries on behalf of EHC to make contact with church leaders and make the work of Every Home Crusade known to them.

I agreed to pray about the matter and give it some thought. The suggestion was challenging and I was excited that I could engage in this work while still carrying on my relief programmes with the UFM. However, I was terrified at the size of the task. I had further consultations with Mr. Allen and Samuel and subsequently agreed to accept the challenge.

The first place EHC suggested I visit was Gabon, which was one of the fields that interested UFM at that time. That first trip and many subsequent visits to different countries in Africa only confirmed my call to Congo over and over again. I was discouraged as I travelled from country to country and saw the slow growth of some churches in comparison to what God was doing in Congo. It helped me to count our blessings that for many years the Congolese have been in charge of their own church administration. Invariably I discovered that where missionaries still 'ran the show' the growth of the church was stunted.

This wider ministry for the EHC not only took me to many French speaking countries in Africa, but opened my eyes to a great potential that would benefit our work in Congo. I was encouraged to find good French literature being produced in Africa, which we could purchase for our Bible Schools in Congo. I also discovered quite a few 'francophone Christian conferences' of which we had had no knowledge. After some negotiations I was able to set this up for our Congolese church leaders who have greatly benefited from this ministry.

While visiting Cameroon, Central African Republic and Ivory Coast, I had many opportunities to meet and discuss various issues with church leaders and speak in some of their meetings. Meeting with missionaries who were working in these countries gave a good insight as to what was happening elsewhere in Africa.

In Ivory Coast it was suggested that I visit a missionary who, after some absence from the country, returned to Abidjan to set up a small printing press. I set off early one morning to find Victor and his print shop. After some time I finally located his whereabouts and was welcomed to the premises. Victor was not available immediately, but while I waited for him I found that the racket of printing presses and folding machines operating was almost unbearable. I wondered how the workers could tolerate the noise level so I paid attention to them as they seemed to be oblivious to the uproar. After only a few minutes I realized they were unaware of the noise for all of them were deaf and only communicated with each other by sign language.

When I met Victor I mentioned that I had observed all his workers seemed to be deaf. He explained that was one of the reasons why he returned to Ivory Coast. He was burdened for this small group of deaf Christians who had no employment. He felt God would have him set up the press and train the group in printing techniques and through them spread the gospel by the printed page. The only person on the staff who could speak besides Victor, was the receptionist. Of course, their audio impairment was helpful in the print shop for they could not hear the deafening din. Besides gospel tracts Victor and his friends were publishing a good range of French books.

The highlight of the visit to Cameroon was meeting with the Korean missionaries. Many years ago the government in Gabon invited Koreans to install a new communication system. Over eighty Koreans arrived in Gabon and after one month in the country they sent word back to Korea saying that the only thing the workers lacked was a pastor. The government paid for a Korean pastor and family to go to Gabon and minister to the Koreans.

Not only did they form a Korean church, but soon the pastor and his team started a Bible School for the young Gabonese in Libreville. That Bible School met a great need in the city and provided evangelists to reach other parts of Gabon with the gospel. When I met with them and explained the work of Every Home Crusade they were so happy that we could supply them with literature for their outreach programme.

The Korean missionaries in Libreville told me that if I ever went to Cameroon I should meet their friends there. I arrived in Yaounde, capital of Cameroon, on a Saturday afternoon. It was not too long after I had left Congo and the noise of war still alarmed me. No one mentioned to me that there would be a national holiday two days after my arrival and this would be marked by a military display. I was staying at the Scripture Union headquarters and that evening I was there alone. The neighbours also seemed to be absent from their home.

Just as darkness fell the army in the military camp nearby decided to practice their air aerobatics ahead of the big event. Suddenly planes roared overhead as they swooped over the military camp. Where I was staying was less than half a mile from there. I was petrified. I thought I had arrived in time to witness another revolutionary coup. I didn't know if these were the rebels or the legitimate forces and there was no one around to ask. The exercise continued for an hour during which time I spent praying for God's protection and looking out of the window. You can imagine how much the neighbours enjoyed the news of my dilemma when they returned home.

Monday was a holiday, but I had already made an appointment with the head of the Protestant schools in the country who was also a pastor. Early that morning I made my way to their headquarters only to discover he was at home. The receptionist telephoned him and he said I should go to his home. That was easier said than done, but I finally found his house where he received me graciously. His wife joined us and after some conversation she produced lunch and I was invited to join them.

Our conversation majored on his concern for the Pygmies in Cameroon who had no contact with the gospel. During our conversation I mentioned Steve Leversedge, a missionary friend in Congo who had organised a training programme in Kinshasa for Pygmy evangelism. I told the pastor that I did not know Steve's address as most likely he had left Kinshasa because of the war. Just then the telephone rang and my host answered the call while I continued to enjoy African food. While I was still eating other guests were shown into the living room, but I had my back to them so could not address them. I was still at the table when the pastor ended his telephone call and apologised to me. Suddenly a voice behind exclaimed, "Is that not Maizie from Kisangani?" I turned around wondering who could know me in Yaounde. It was Steve Leversedge whose name I had just mentioned to the pastor. He had recently moved to Yaounde and someone had told him that this pastor was interested in Pygmy evangelism. God's ways are beyond knowing. As I had proved on countless other occasions, God's ways and timing are perfect.

During the following days in Cameroon I met with many choice servants of God who were so dedicated in their work for Christ. Among these were my Korean friends who were building a Bible Seminary and a new church. They were people of vision and energy for God's work. The visit also had its disappointments. I went to a seminary to introduce the EHC literature. Evangelical teachers had founded this seminary, but it had drifted from the fundamentals of the faith and was now very much in the liberal camp. When I presented the EHC literature to the Dean he said they would have little need for our literature. When I asked about evangelism classes he told me they did not really major on evangelism at their seminary. That was one of the saddest statements I have ever heard.

While in Cameroon I felt constrained to visit the Central African Republic (CAR). Missionaries told me that it would be virtually impossible to obtain a visa for CAR within a few days. I had seen God do impossibilities before so I decided I would push the door. Next morning I went to the CAR embassy. When a secretary finally appeared she told me I would have to wait eight days for a visa. The lady was very pleasant and as she spoke I noticed she had the same features as those who live in North-Eastern Congo. I wondered if she could she be from that region. I expressed my sadness at having to wait eight days, but instead of speaking French I spoke to her in Lingala. She was amazed at a white woman speaking Lingala. Soon she was in full flow in Lingala asking me where was I from; what was I doing and how did I know Lingala? The result of it all was that I had my visa that afternoon.

I should have arrived in CAR in the morning, but the flight was delayed until late evening. Because of the delay I doubted if anyone would be there to meet me. As the passengers disembarked at Bangui, I looked around the plane and discerned that several other whites 'looked like missionaries.' My discernment was right and soon I was on a taxi-bus which had come to meet some workers from the Brethren Mission.

I had a worthwhile time in CAR with many showing interest in the EHC literature. For my return flight I was due to check in at 11.00 a.m., but there was no petrol in Bangui and there almost was a fight for a secure taxi. Early that morning a young fellow at the gate of the guesthouse asked one of his taxi friends to come and pick me up at 10.45 a.m. and take me to the airport.

At about 10.30 a.m. I went to the guesthouse office to pay my bill and as I entered a missionary flopped into a chair as if he was absolutely exhausted. I learned he had just arrived from the United States via Ivory Coast and for that reason he was very tired. We introduced ourselves to each other whereupon I also discovered he had worked in another part of Congo and said he had heard my name 'somewhere.'

While paying my bill the lady at the desk asked this new arrival what his business was. He said he was Director of Evangelism Explosion and had come to organise a trip for an evangelistic team going to Cameroon for a conference. He asked the lady for directions to the Bible Society, as he wanted to find copies of John's Gospel to use in their work. At that the lady spoke up and said, "You need to look no further for that is why Maizie is here".

I had only five minutes before I was due to leave and he had only arrived five minutes earlier. In that short time we were able to help Evangelism Explosion with a supply of the Gospel of John for their work. After that he ordered twenty-four thousand copies of John's Gospel for Gabon and other orders are to follow.

I left Bangui with a song in my heart for all the Lord had enabled me to do in four days in CAR and the many people He had allowed to cross my path. I was also thankful for His protection while travelling in rattling taxis, unreliable planes, and dodging dangerous and, at times, reckless drivers while crossing roads in unfamiliar places.

After each trip to Africa I returned to Mr. Allen and Samuel with orders for millions of tracts and tens of thousands of booklets. For weeks and months after my return I received letters and e-mails soliciting Every Home Crusade to help supply literature for their churches too.

On one of my trips to Kampala, I had to stop off in Nairobi. The plane for Kampala was due to leave the next morning so I joined up with two African friends for coffee at a local café that afternoon to catch up on all their news. While we were drinking and chatting a man approached our table. He was African so I sat back to allow him to speak to the friends, but he pointed his finger at me and said, "I wish to speak with you."

I had never seen this man before, but he produced one of my business cards from Every Home Crusade. I asked him where he got it and he told me that he was from Cameroon and had seen my picture when he returned home. He pastored one of the principal churches in the area and was keen that we should supply them with literature. One never knows who is watching or whom we will meet.

After several trips for EHC I reverted to making a few visits to Congo. So many orders for French literature arrived from Africa following my visits that the printing team was glad of a break so that they could attend to requests from other parts of the world.

28

Every Home in Africa

I was driving down the main motorway between my home and Belfast on my way to speak at a ladies' meeting. Earlier that day I had been at the Every Home Crusade office where Samuel Adams suggested I should think of paying visits to Togo, Burkina Faso and Benin, all in the west of Africa. However, I was not feeling very confident about the trip and as I made my way to the meeting I expressed my doubts to the Lord.

The meeting went very well, but during the closing hymn God spoke to my heart. I sang the familiar hymn like I never had sung it before, "Anywhere with Jesus I can safely go." I felt my reservations about the trip were legitimate. I was heading off into the unknown and to three countries where I did not know anyone; at least I didn't think I knew anyone. All hesitance was swept away by the time we reached the end of that hymn and during the drive home that night I was already formulating plans for the trip to West Africa.

I arrived in Lome, the capital of Togo, late on the Saturday and made my way to prearranged accommodation in a self-catering guesthouse. Because I didn't have any local currency I had great difficulty persuading a nearby shop owner to sell me bread, milk and a few other basic essentials.

The following morning, Sunday, there was no one else in the guesthouse and the guard did not speak French so I did not know what to do or where to go. I did what I instinctively do in such predicaments, I prayed and asked the Lord to direct me for I was there to do His work. After that word of prayer I walked to the main road where I hailed a taxi and agreed a price with him to take me to the nearest Baptist Church. The fare was only about £0.30 so I knew he was not making too big a killing out of me. In fact, he didn't know of any Baptist churches in Lome for he was a Muslim, so he took me to the Catholic Chapel.

I tried to explain to him that this was not the right church so he called to a lady on the street to ask directions. I could hardly believe what I heard when she said she was going to the Baptist Church. I was already late. Most Sunday morning services in Africa begin at 9.00 a.m. and it was now 9.15 a.m. However, the lady told me their service started at 8.00 a.m. We were even later than I thought.

At the Baptist Church I was ushered all the way to the front row and took my place just as the Church secretary was making the announcements. All guests were asked to stand and introduce themselves. This gave me a welcome opportunity to say who I was and why I was in Lome.

I hoped to speak to the pastor after the service and inquire if there was an Alliance of Evangelical churches in Lome and where I might find their offices. Even later than my arrival, a man arrived and took his seat next to me at the front of the church. During the offering the stranger spoke to me and asked who I was and why I was in Lome. During the interaction that followed I discovered that he was the man I was looking for, the secretary of the Alliance of Evangelical churches in Togo. Why do I ever doubt God when He is so faithful and unerring?

Following the service we stayed behind to talk for a while and he gave me many names and addresses of local people I should contact. Armed with the names and addresses I left early Monday to present the literature ministry of EHC to various Christian leaders. I soon discovered that the work regime in Togo is a little irregular.

The general population work from 8.00 a.m. to 12.00 noon and then rest until 3.00 p.m. after which they return to work until 5.30 or 6.00 p.m. It was most inconvenient to have to return five kilometres from the centre of town to the guesthouse at noon every day.

At Praise Chapel I met the church director who was most friendly and helpful. It was obvious he had a deep concern for reaching others with the gospel as he spoke of the work the church members and Bible School students were doing in the city. I thought he was somewhat discouraged in this work but when I mentioned this, he told me the following story. A fellow arrived at their church who was curious to find out what went on there. After several visits he indicated he would like to become a follower of Jesus Christ whereupon the pastor led him to Christ. The new convert continued to attend all the meetings and in the prayer meetings he would pray for his family back home in his village on the Ghanaian border.

One day he approached the pastor and asked if the Church would send someone to preach the gospel back in his village. The man said he was willing to help pay for a car to take them there. After some discussion and prayer the church finally decided to set up a visit to the man's home region. The pastor accompanied three church elders and discovered the village was in a very remote location.

They took a vehicle part of the way, but had to leave it and walk for miles before they reached this village. The new convert had already sent word ahead of the impending visit so the whole population was waiting to receive the delegation from Praise Chapel. Afterwards, the pastor confessed he had never seen such a sight. Village chiefs and all the people suspended their activities for four days during which he and the elders preached the gospel. God did a great work in the remote community and many of the people said they wanted to turn to Christ.

As they prepared to make the return trip one of the elders refused to leave the village. When asked why his reply was, "I will not return to Lome with you. I will stay here and teach these people God's Word. We cannot leave them without any teaching"

The elder did stay on and the director told me that there is a thriving church in that village today, and not only there, but in many surrounding villages of that region. The director himself had only arrived in Lome about one year earlier as a missionary from Nigeria and went home for one week once every three months to see his wife and children. Now the family was coming to join him in Lome. He had come in advance in order to have time to learn French before his family would come. Such is the dedication by many of these national missionaries.

The Lord had another surprise in store for me that day. We called at a local radio station and the station manager said he would see us in ten minutes. Eventually we were ushered into this very plush office where we found an executive surrounded by papers. I soon found out the manager was a lawyer and from this office he ran his business. The radio and television studios were behind his offices. From across his desk he began to share his testimony with me. "When I was eight years old my parents became Jehovah Witnesses. I went with them to the Kingdom Hall although I never thought of their faith for myself. I finished school and trained as a high school teacher. I married, but soon we discovered that my wife could not bear children. We began looking for a solution, whether with 'white man's' medicine or with local herbs."

"One day a pastor arrived and when my wife told him of her infertility he prayed that God would give us a child. Sure enough, by next year, my wife gave birth. When it came to the 'naming ceremony' the pastor asked me to pray for something definite from the Lord and God would answer. I asked God to give me financial blessings and if He did I would build a church.

"I was studying law at the time and after obtaining my Master's degree became an attorney. The Lord answered prayer and I became rich. Unfortunately, I forgot my vow and I began living the high life, moving with sophisticated girls, drinking, buying executive cars and building large houses to make lots of money. A year after becoming an attorney I became very sick. The doctors gave me all sorts of medicines, but to no avail. One day my friends took me to see the pastor who had prayed with my wife and for the first time I understood what my sins were and how Jesus could forgive my sins. That day I confessed my sins to God and asked the Lord Jesus into my life. God touched me that day and I was changed.

"The pastor reminded me of the vow I had made some time ago when our child had been named. I bought some land and built the Baptist Gospel Church of Lome. After the inauguration of the church I was completely healed. Since that day God has helped me in so many ways and it is a joy to be able to serve Him. I have since been able to build fifteen churches, but today, rather than build buildings, I want to concentrate on spreading the good news. That is why I have purchased and outfitted two buses in which evangelists travel from village to village spreading the gospel. We have opened three radio stations and one television station here in Lome and run a medical centre, a missionary school and a home for the down and outs. I also head up a co-operative bank which helps our work. God is good to us and I only want to please Him in my life."

He then went on to tell me that because he left witchcraft and a Masonic-like society, he lost quite a few former clients, but he was not worried about that as God had provided many other clients and through his legal work he was able to finance the various works.

We further spoke of the spread of Islam in Togo and how governments impose high taxes on the Christian radio stations in the hope that this would discourage them from spreading the gospel.

I found the man so refreshing and it was evident he was 'burning out' for God. When I shared with him the work of Every Home Crusade and how we could help him with evangelistic and follow-up literature he said that it was an answer to his prayers.

After four days in Togo I flew to Ouagadougou, capital of Burkina Faso. As I checked in at Lome airport I was able to meet up with Ed Morrow who was on his way to Abidjan. Ed and Hilde now work for Samaritan's Purse and he was in Togo to survey their programme there. For an hour we were able to catch up on news of mutual interest.

It is such a joy to walk with the Lord and to see Him handling every situation. From Lome I had made a telephone call to make a reservation at the guesthouse in Ouagadougou and ask them to collect me at the airport. They told me they did not offer that service. We were due to land at 9.30 p.m., but as usual, we were just

' a little bit late' and arrived in at 11.30 p.m. The flight offered 'free seating' which meant that you could sit anywhere in the cabin.

I fell into the first vacant row after being told that I must put my hand luggage into the plane's hold. There was no way I was going to part with my computer so I stubbornly wrestled with it under the seat. Soon a lady arrived beside me with four bags, all larger than mine, and it was obvious she knew the stewardesses. Soon we were talking and she told me she had been in Togo as her mother had died there recently. I discovered the lady was a member of the Assembly of God Church in Ouagadougou. Quite out of the blue she asked me who was meeting me at the airport and when I said I planned to take a taxi she gave me a fifteen-minute lecture on how unsafe the taxis were in Ouagadougou. After the lecture she asked where I was staying. When I told her about the guesthouse she immediately said they were passing by there and would leave me to the door. Again I found the Lord is always one step ahead.

Although it was almost midnight when we touched down in Ouagadougou, the temperature outside was 39°. The guard on duty at the guesthouse gate had an envelope with my name. It contained the key to my room. Inside the bedroom it seemed even hotter than at the airport and it never cooled off the whole week I was in town. I drank gallons of water and kept a fan going continually, but this was of little use for it was only circulating hot air. It was mango and strawberry season in Burkina Faso so I bought a plentiful supply and in my room I had a good plate of fruit each morning for breakfast while I bought dinner in a local restaurant.

I had many good contacts in the city and met with a lot of enthusiasm for EHC literature. I am often humbled when I meet people who are so sold out to the Lord in spite of having little of this world's goods. One blind man walked forty kilometres to try to secure literature for his outreach. He was an amazing man. Although blind, he had started an orphanage many years earlier and this now housed more than one hundred and forty children. Someone had told him about EHC and that I was in the city so he asked one of the young boys from the orphanage to accompany him to the city. I was not only glad to meet him, but also to be able to help in his ministry.

Perhaps the high point of my time in Burkina Faso was meeting a couple from Tear Fund, Belgium, who were working with street children. One young lad who had been a Christian for a year started a Bible study in his school and asked the missionary if I could provide him with copies of the Gospel of John for all his class. The couple had rescued thirty-five children from Ouagadougou's streets and provided accommodation for them in a hostel and helped supplement their education. They were also working closely with seventy other families whose children had become involved in street problems.

I am aware that I face risky situations while visiting some of these African republics and cities where I am not too sure of the safe areas. Before leaving Burkina Faso I went to reconfirm my flight at the airline office in the city centre. On my way there a man began to follow me. After ten minutes he was still on my heels and I tried to lose him in the crowd. No matter where I turned he kept turning up close behind. I noticed two schoolgirls walking in the same direction on the other side of the street so I crossed over and asked them where they were going. They said they were on their way to the Cathedral. I knew the airline office was beside the Cathedral so I explained why I would like to walk with them. Even with my new companions the man did not seem to be put off and soon turned up again. Having some support, I stopped to confront the man and gave him a piece of my mind. The older of the two girls also told him to clear off so he withdrew. Incidents like this remind me that He cares for us and our safety comes from Him.

I arrived in Cotonou, capital of Benin, a little late but they were one hour behind Burkina Faso so that helped. I was told to take a taxi to the guesthouse which was supposed to be near the airport. When I emerged out of the arrival lounge I was confronted by almost fifty teenagers offering taxi rides. I saw an older man and thought it wiser to travel with him. After striking the right price I was taken to a taxi car, only to find it driven by a young lad. It had rained heavily before I arrived and the road was flooded in many places. When I saw the boy behind the steering wheel and imagined the slippery state of the roads I took a fit of giggling and said to myself, *Only in Africa.*

With my baggage in the boot, the driver removed a wet plastic bag from the passenger seat which was used to keep it dry from the water that poured in through the roof. The window on my side of the boneshaker would neither open nor close so, as we splashed through muddy puddles, I had an unwelcome, but free shower. One headlight was at full beam and one wiper only wiped a part of the windscreen. How he saw where he was going was a miracle but he did not seem concerned. The most important thing to him was that his radio played at top volume. I only wished I had a video to record the reckless drive and miraculous arrival at my destination.

I have travelled to many cities all over Africa, but I have never seen traffic anywhere like that in Cotonou. I soon discovered that the cheapest and fastest way to get around the city was to hire a motorbike and a driver. At nearly all the traffic lights about sixty motorbikes of every size, shape and noise, were poised as if it was the start of a Grand Prix. As soon as the lights changed everyone beeped their horns and off they went. It seemed to be great for the motorcycle riders, but I assure you it was terrifying for a pillion passenger.

As I walked up a street I saw a white man exiting from a Land Rover on the side of which was a logo marked, 'Mercy Ships'. I stopped with him to explain why I was in Cotonou and if their ship might be interested in EHC literature. He told me there were about four hundred people living on the ship, but he was the person responsible for the literature for their evangelistic programme. I visited the ship and found it most interesting. Locals received medical treatment free of charge. They had many specialised personnel for complicated surgeries including those who operated a cataract clinic.

Jacob, the leader of the Bible Study groups in Cotonou University heard that I had arrived with Christian literature and came to visit me at the guesthouse. The young man devoted all his time to the work among the students. He told me how he was raised in a Catholic home and went through all the religious ritual of his church. After school Jacob left for University where he met different religious groups, but was especially drawn to the voodoo schools. He told me that 60% of the university students have allegiance to animistic gods. After being involved in voodoo for some time someone gave him a gospel tract. He read it over and over again and finally searched out the student who had given the tract to him. As a result he sought God's forgiveness and yielded His life to the Lord Jesus.

During the week he attended the University Bible Study, but at weekends he tried to fulfil his responsibilities towards his mother church. He found this to be very unsatisfactory. After discussing his problem with student friends he read the tract which taught that he needed to attend a church where Christ was presented as the only way of salvation. It was then that the light finally dawned on him how much he needed the fellowship of those who enjoyed like precious faith.

After he qualified as a teacher Jacob went on to teach in several colleges, but could never forget what God had taught him through the written word. As a result he dedicated his life to leading Bible studies and organising evangelistic events for students. When I shared with him the work of EHC he just kept thanking God for the possibility of having copies of the Gospel of John to give to these students.

Jacob was only one of several interesting people I met in Cotonou. I travelled from Cotonou to Lome by taxi on what they told me would be a four-hour journey. I sat in the front seat of the Peugeot 306 with four Africans squeezed into the back seat. It was a very hot morning when we set out and had only driven sixteen kilometres when a sudden surge of heat began to come from the engine. The driver stopped abruptly when he saw a rather hefty lady carrying several bags make her way towards the car. I knew that the only place for her was to share the seat with me, but I was at a loss to see how it could be done. I had been told that if I wanted the front seat to myself I would have to pay for two people. Seeing what might happen I swallowed my Ballymena reputation and suddenly became quite extravagant. I paid the driver for an extra place and was much relieved when he drove off and left the woman behind. The total cost was only £6.00 so I didn't feel too bad.

I could tell by their dress that the people in the rear seat were Muslims. When I discovered that the officials at the border were Muslims also, I just tagged along with my fellow passengers. As a result I got my passport stamped without any problem. The crossing at the actual border post was an unforgettable experience. People were roasting goats and chickens right there and offering meals to those crossing the border in both directions. Against the background of crowds of people milling around and a cacophony of noise from hens, roosters and goats, travellers kept shouting at the officials, "Am I next?" I was glad when we finally made it across the border into Togo.

On the dashboard of the taxi was written: "Maximum Speed 60 kph." The taxi driver took that as his minimum speed and used his horn constantly for at least one third of the journey. When I finally dismounted from the taxi several hours later, I was almost a nervous wreck. Time did not concern me. I was just glad to have arrived in one piece and gave thanks to the Lord for the fine work His angels had done to protect us. It really was a miracle!

The greater miracle was to follow. Tons of EHC literature followed to these West African countries and through the paper-missionaries and copies of the Gospel of John, thousands of lives have been touched. This has been a ministry of casting our bread upon the waters and in the eternal tabernacles of glory we shall see the miracles of grace which resulted from this work of faith.

29

Dark Clouds and Blue Skies

Congo is in the heart of Africa. It is a land of blue skies, lush green forests, immense mineral wealth and great people. Sounds idyllic? It should be, but alas, dark clouds hang over the land today; much of its vast mineral wealth has been plundered; the forests have been stained by crimson Congolese blood spilled in successive revolutions; and the Congolese people long for something better than what they have experienced until now.

During twenty-four years in Congo I have seen many a good day ruined by the invasion of dark clouds laden with rain. When those clouds come, they blot out the sun, transform the forest from a verdant green to a misty grey, turn roads into rivers of mud and cause the people to run for shelter. However, clouds transport rain and that rain plays its part in invigorating forest and grasslands and plains.

Sadly there are other clouds over Congo today.

Political clouds are dark and threatening. Congo has been raped, butchered and looted by various forces purporting to operate in the name of a political ideology. Independent reports put the number of people killed during the last four years at 2.5 million. That is equal to wiping out the entire population of Northern Ireland or Wales. Within the last two weeks at this time of writing, an estimated one thousand people were massacred in Nyankunde and the Mission Hospital there was totally destroyed. Rebel groups backed by neighbouring countries, fight for their right to govern Congo. Many analysts see the aggression and counter-aggression between parties in power and those who want to be in power as a war for wealth and who can control and capitalize on the country's vast mineral resources. No one knows when these clouds of war will blow away.

Economic clouds impose grim conditions for those who are caught beneath their sombre shadows. Besides much of the economy going up in smoke with the war effort, the gross national product is abysmally low, industries have ceased to operate in the large cities and towns and multiple thousands of previously employed people are now jobless. Unemployment not only robs the worker of a wage, but a family of a livelihood. This might mean that for every worker made redundant, up to ten or twelve people are in jeopardy of destitution.

The vicious-circle redundant industry, unemployment and soaring inflation only dissipate the inevitable scant supply of basic essentials. In Kisangani, with an estimated population of up to one million people, prices of available goods are almost prohibitive for ordinary people. Rural people suffer when invading soldiers help themselves to the ripening crops of hard-working families. In this grave economic climate stealing is rampant.

There is a great cloud hanging over the Congolese church. The church is not exempt from trouble during an economic crisis. While people continue to flock daily to hear God's Word yet they have little or nothing to give as an offering other than the praise of their hearts. Those who do give usually contribute the smallest denomination of Congolese currency, five hundred of which equal £1. Therefore, pastors and evangelists live in poverty as they care for congregations, which also go hungry and have no prospect of earning money. In the prevailing conditions pastors are exceptionally busy conducting funerals, visiting sick and helping those who are in prison, often unjustly.

Do you understand when I say that a hungry and busy pastor finds little time to read and study God's Word? Consequently, there is a paucity of systematic Bible teaching in the churches and into this gap many false cults make inroads and grow numerically all over Africa. This is made worse by reason of many of our young people never having an opportunity to go to school and because they cannot read, they become vulnerable fodder to these predators of error.

Perhaps the most troublesome clouds are those which descend like mist, hindering visibility and bringing life to a standstill. I feel that is where we are in our missionary endeavour. Many questions are being asked of those of us who have been called by God to serve Him in Congo; *What do we do in such troubled times? Where should we begin? What of tomorrow?* The present generation is growing up without education and we wonder where will we find nurses, doctors, pastors, evangelists and teachers to serve the population. Mist has descended upon us and it is hard to see the way ahead. My heart breaks for my friends in Congo, but I feel so helpless.

These are the dark clouds over Congo today. Missionary Aviation Fellowship does a sterling work for churches all over Congo. Often when the pilot calls on the radio at the beginning of a busy day, he wants to know what the weather is like on route and at his destination. If it is a cloudy morning a later weather report is needed. No matter how cloudy it is in our part of Congo, it is a very rare occurrence if there is no blue sky. I can still hear the pilot ask, "Are there no breaks in the clouds? In which direction is the blue sky?"

Thank God dark clouds don't last forever. Before long the blue sky will be breaking through and sunlight will bathe the countryside. In spite of the metaphorical clouds I have mentioned, I am glad that the blue sky is breaking through all over Congo and soon the Sun of Righteousness will shine brightly upon our beloved land.

I see the blue sky of our training programmes. Today we have more applications for young people wanting to go to Bible School than ever before. It is not an easy job for a church to choose three or four candidates to send to Bible School when they have more than eighty who would like to go.

Our nursing training programme at the Mission Hospital in Nyankunde has more candidates than we can cope with. It costs a lot to send students seven hundred kilometres from Kisangani to the hospital in Nyankunde and help maintain them during their four years of training. It is not just the financial commitment of these families to support a son or a daughter in Nyankunde, but also coping with the absence of a young boy when he was the one expected to provide sustenance for others.

The decision to go for training is not easy for the candidates either. One of our male nurses had five children, three girls and two boys. His wife died when the children were still quite young. Eventually the three girls got married, but the two boys decided to study to be nurses like their father. The family planned that after the two boys finished their secondary education, the younger would plant fields to pay for the education of the older brother and when the older qualified, he in turn would support his younger brother. The first boy arrived at the university and worked and studied very conscientiously and was one of only ten students who passed the first year exams. During his time at university he worked for me in the evenings and this gave him enough money to buy a return ticket to visit his father and younger brother during the holidays.

On his first trip home he got a ride on a truck. On the eighth day of the four-hundred kilometre journey he was only a few kilometres from home, but felt so hungry he decided to buy a meal of cooked fish and ugali (a thick porridge made from cassava flour) from a roadside vendor. It is always risky buying food in these unhygienic booths and tragically, because of the meal, he developed food poisoning and only survived a few hours after reaching home. His family, who had sacrificed so much, was totally devastated. His younger brother was not only shattered by his brother's sudden death, but their plans to help in each other's education had been dashed. The young man searched his heart to know what he should do. In spite of the tragedy, his father encouraged him to go and study and trust God to provide for him.

God did just that. At the back of his small rented room in a mud hut in Kisangani, he kept rabbits and ducks. Whenever his rent was due he generally paid with livestock. On the day the rebels arrived and swarmed all over town he came to my house carrying his precious rabbits and ducks and asked if I could possibly hide them or they would be stolen from his hut.

I had no place for his livestock, but we soon worked out a way to keep them safe. God continued to provide for this young man and today he is a qualified nurse in one of our dispensaries. Unfortunately his father did not live long enough to see his son qualify. The price of education in Congo is not to be measured in purely monetary value; families pay a very high cost.

Blue sky is also making a hole in the clouds by the vision of many of our younger trained men. One student, Lilenga, recently graduated from seminary and he has the vision of reaching Kisangani by radio. He discovered that the national radio station offers a half-hour of broadcasting time weekly at a very reasonable price. His prayer request was that God would open a way so that many sick people who sit on their grass mats, too weak and hungry to work, will have the opportunity to hear the gospel.

God also gave a vision to Lilongo and Asongi of going into the Pygmy forest and reaching these neglected people for the Lord. Asemaga, who was trained as a Christian Educator wants to set up a Christian education centre to teach others also.

A gift from a group in Ireland provided a bicycle for a senior pastor who had responsibility for a group of churches. In six months he was able to visit all sixty-one churches under his supervision. In many of these congregations there are evangelists and elders who teach God's Word. He feels so blessed because he has a bicycle, which means he is able go to where the evangelists and elders are and bring them together for teaching sessions. It was in that area that we conducted an evangelistic campaign four years ago. In an appeal for help the pastor explained to me that about 50% of those churches have no Scriptures other than the Gospel of John booklets which were printed by EHC and distributed by us four years ago. Because they have no other Scriptures the pastor tries to limit his preaching to the Gospel of John so that the congregation can follow.

The blue sky of God's faithfulness causes the warmth of His Son's love and grace to shine through in spite of the angry clouds of war and inhumanity. Nothing surprises our Sovereign Lord. His plan is perfect.

Many of the village people are Christians and when the Ugandan army overran their villages they took refuge in the forest. For twenty-three months they eked out a meagre existence. They survived by eating berries and wild fruit and hunting animals. With bamboo and large leaves they erected crude shacks for shelter, but these gave little protection from the heavy rains or wild animals.

When news reached the forest that the Ugandan army had left their villages thousands of these forest refugees began to return home. Slowly and fearfully they emerged from the forest only to discover that the fleeing army had burned all their homes to the ground. Village after village was totally razed, but these dogged people began to rebuild their stick and mud homes again.

The pastors had lived with the village people while they hid in the forest and worked alongside them to reconstruct their homes. However, one day they were summoned to a meeting of the village chiefs. They sat and listened to the chiefs communicate to them that the people did not want them to build any churches in the villages just yet. In African culture it is rude to interrupt a speaker or to ask a question while he is still in the middle of his discourse. It is always good manners to listen until the person speaking has finished.

While the dejected pastors listened patiently to the chiefs addressing them, they were wondering why all this was happening. Soon it became clear. During their enforced exile in the forest the villagers' garments had rotted. Some who had more than one piece of cloth had hidden what they had in a hole in the ground. However, when they emerged from the forest they discovered that the hidden clothes had also rotted even though they had been secured in plastic bags. The people were dressed in virtual rags and felt they could not go into God's house dressed so shabbily.

The chiefs went on to explain that the people were wanting the pastors to simply build a pulpit large enough to support two small lamps and a place to set the Bible. They wanted the portable pulpit to be placed in an open space where people could sit around at night and listen to the pastor preach God's Word. In that way people would not see their neighbours or what he or she was wearing. The chiefs ended their appeal by saying "Hold the services as the sun begins to set on Sunday evenings and let us sing our praises to Him then. Likewise, set the time of the early morning prayer meeting before sunrise so that no one will see the poor state of his neighbour's garb."

God is blessing and building His Church in Congo. The blue sky of heaven is prevailing over the dark clouds of hell, and will prevail, until the Sun of Righteousness arises with healing in His wings.